NATHANIEL
HAWTHORNE

COMPREHENSIVE RESEARCH
AND STUDY GUIDE

BLOOM'S
MAJOR
NOVELISTS

**EDITED AND WITH AN
INTRODUCTION BY HAROLD BLOOM**

BLOOM'S MAJOR DRAMATISTS

Anton Chekhov
Henrik Ibsen
Arthur Miller
Eugene O'Neill
Shakespeare's Comedies
Shakespeare's Histories
Shakespeare's Romances
Shakespeare's Tragedies
George Bernard Shaw
Tennessee Williams

BLOOM'S MAJOR NOVELISTS

Jane Austen
The Brontës
Willa Cather
Charles Dickens
William Faulkner
F. Scott Fitzgerald
Nathaniel Hawthorne
Ernest Hemingway
Toni Morrison
John Steinbeck
Mark Twain
Alice Walker

BLOOM'S MAJOR SHORT STORY WRITERS

William Faulkner
F. Scott Fitzgerald
Ernest Hemingway
O. Henry
James Joyce
Herman Melville
Flannery O'Connor
Edgar Allan Poe
J. D. Salinger
John Steinbeck
Mark Twain
Eudora Welty

BLOOM'S MAJOR WORLD POETS

Geoffrey Chaucer
Emily Dickinson
John Donne
T. S. Eliot
Robert Frost
Langston Hughes
John Milton
Edgar Allan Poe
Shakespeare's Poems & Sonnets
Alfred, Lord Tennyson
Walt Whitman
William Wordsworth

BLOOM'S NOTES

The Adventures of Huckleberry Finn
Aeneid
The Age of Innocence
Animal Farm
The Autobiography of Malcolm X
The Awakening
Beloved
Beowulf
Billy Budd, Benito Cereno, & Bartleby the Scrivener
Brave New World
The Catcher in the Rye
Crime and Punishment
The Crucible

Death of a Salesman
A Farewell to Arms
Frankenstein
The Grapes of Wrath
Great Expectations
The Great Gatsby
Gulliver's Travels
Hamlet
Heart of Darkness & The Secret Sharer
Henry IV, Part One
I Know Why the Caged Bird Sings
Iliad
Inferno
Invisible Man
Jane Eyre
Julius Caesar

King Lear
Lord of the Flies
Macbeth
A Midsummer Night's Dream
Moby-Dick
Native Son
Nineteen Eighty-Four
Odyssey
Oedipus Plays
Of Mice and Men
The Old Man and the Sea
Othello
Paradise Lost
The Portrait of a Lady
A Portrait of the Artist as a Young Man

Pride and Prejudice
The Red Badge of Courage
Romeo and Juliet
The Scarlet Letter
Silas Marner
The Sound and the Fury
The Sun Also Rises
A Tale of Two Cities
Tess of the D'Urbervilles
Their Eyes Were Watching God
To Kill a Mockingbird
Uncle Tom's Cabin
Wuthering Heights

NATHANIEL HAWTHORNE

COMPREHENSIVE RESEARCH
AND STUDY GUIDE

BLOOM'S

MAJOR
NOVELISTS

EDITED AND WITH AN INTRODUCTION
BY HAROLD BLOOM

First Printing
1 3 5 7 9 8 6 4 2

Library of Congress Cataloging-in-Publication Data
Nathaniel Hawthorne / edited and with an introduction by Harold Bloom.
       p.   cm. — (Bloom's major novelists)
    Includes bibliographical references and index.
    ISBN 0-7910-5253-2 (hc)
    1. Hawthorne, Nathaniel, 1804–1864—Examinations—Study guides.
I. Bloom, Harold. II. Series
    PS1888.N295   1999
    813'.3—dc21   99–23593
                                                CIP

Chelsea House Publishers
1974 Sproul Road, Suite 400
Broomall, PA 19008-0914

The Chelsea House WorldWide Web address is
www.chelseahouse.com

Contributing Editor: Gwendolyn Bellerman

Contents

User's Guide

This volume is designed to present biographical, critical, and bibliographical information on the author's best-known or most important works. Following Harold Bloom's editor's note and introduction are a detailed biography of the author, discussing major life events and important literary accomplishments. A plot summary of each novel follows, tracing significant themes, patterns, and motifs in the work.

A selection of critical extracts, derived from previously published material from leading critics, analyzes aspects of each work. The extracts consist of statements from the author, if available, early reviews of the work, and later evaluations up to the present. A bibliography of the author's writings (including a complete list of all works written, cowritten, edited, and translated), a list of additional books and articles on the author and his or her work, and an index of themes and ideas in the author's writings conclude the volume.

～

Harold Bloom is Sterling Professor of the Humanities at Yale University and Henry W. and Albert A. Berg Professor of English at the New York University Graduate School. He is the author of over 20 books and the editor of more than 30 anthologies of literary criticism.

Professor Bloom's works include *Shelley's Mythmaking* (1959), *The Visionary Company* (1961), *Blake's Apocalypse* (1963), *Yeats* (1970), *A Map of Misreading* (1975), *Kabbalah and Criticism* (1975), and *Agon: Toward a Theory of Revisionism* (1982). *The Anxiety of Influence* (1973) sets forth Professor Bloom's provocative theory of the literary relationships between the great writers and their predecessors. His most recent books include *The American Religion* (1992), *The Western Canon* (1994), *Omens of Millennium: The Gnosis of Angels, Dreams, and Resurrection* (1996), and *Shakespeare: The Invention of the Human* (1998), a finalist for the 1998 National Book Award.

Professor Bloom earned his Ph.D. from Yale University in 1955 and has served on the Yale faculty since then. He is a 1985 MacArthur Foundation Award recipient, served as the Charles Eliot Norton Professor of Poetry at Harvard University in 1987–88, and has received honorary degrees from the universities of Rome and Bologna. In 1999, Professor Bloom received the prestigious American Academy of Arts and Letters Gold Medal for Criticism.

Currently, Harold Bloom is the editor of numerous Chelsea House volumes of literary criticism, including the series BLOOM'S NOTES, BLOOM'S MAJOR SHORT STORY WRITERS, BLOOM'S MAJOR POETS, MAJOR LITERARY CHARACTERS, MODERN CRITICAL VIEWS, MODERN CRITICAL INTERPRETATIONS, AND WOMEN WRITERS OF ENGLISH AND THEIR WORKS.

Editor's Note

The copious Critical Views presented here on Hawthorne's three major novels give us some thirty different perspectives upon his achievement. I single out, for particular mention, Henry James and Michael Colacurcio on *The Scarlet Letter;* Michael Davitt Bell and Michael T. Gilmore on *The House of the Seven Gables;* and R. W. B. Lewis, Nina Baym, and Evan Carton on *The Marble Faun.*

Introduction

HAROLD BLOOM

The lonely art of Nathaniel Hawthorne remains one of the cultural monuments of our nation. It continues to provide for the deepest imaginative needs of the solitary reader, of whatever country. Hawthorne's vision of reality remains unsurpassed, short of Shakespeare and Dante. *The Scarlet Letter* and *The Marble Faun* trouble the heart and stimulate the intellect. As Herman Melville and Henry James testified, Hawthorne is a marvelously subtle storyteller and revealer of the soul. Only James himself and William Faulkner ultimately challenge Hawthorne as *the* American novelist (despite some remarkable tales, Melville remains the author of the one prose epic, *Moby-Dick,* rather than a novelist as such, and Mark Twain abides primarily as the genial sage of *Huckleberry Finn,* most American of all narratives.)

Rereading *The Scarlet Letter* always constitutes a lesson in how to read and why. A procession of extraordinary representations of women has followed after Hester Prynne in American literature, yet even the strongest—Isabel Archer in James's *The Portrait of a Lady* and Ántonia in Willa Cather's *My Ántonia*—do not match Hester Prynne in her aesthetic and cultural reverberations. For Hester *is,* in many ways, the American Eve, the Emersonian vision that atones for our lack of any adequate representation of the American Adam. Like Milton's own Eve, Hester is far superior to her fate, and imaginatively preferable to Adam's (and Milton's) God. Hawthorne subtly conveys Hester's sexual power to us, with far less ambivalence than Milton manifests in celebrating Eve's sexual strength. Sensual and tragic, Hester is larger than her book and her world, because her greatness of spirit, like her heroic sexuality, is ill-served by the terrible alternatives of the Satanic Chillingworth (Iago's understudy) and the timid Dimmesdale, an absurdly inadequate adulterous lover for the sublime Hester.

Hester's Self-Reliance is her authentic religion, and it enables her to survive the outrages of societal ostracism and erotic repression. As critics rightly point out, Hester is herself an artist, whose work as embroiderer parallels Hawthorne's own art as romancer. Can we not call Hester Hawthorne's Muse or Interior Paramour (to employ a fine phrase of Wallace Stevens)? As such Hester exerts a fierce pressure upon Hawthorne himself, compelling him to abandon romance for the psychological novel, almost despite his own preferences.

Even *The Marble Faun*, so much prophecy of the novel of Americans abroad, from Henry James and Edith Wharton through Hemingway and Scott Fitzgerald, is not quite of the eminence of *The Scarlet Letter*. There are only a dozen or so of essential American literary classics, including *Moby-Dick* and *Huckleberry Finn*, Emerson's essays and Thoreau's *Walden*, Whitman's *Leaves of Grass* and Emily Dickinson's poems, James's *The Portrait of a Lady* and Faulkner's *As I Lay Dying*, the poems of Wallace Stevens and Hart Crane, and Cormac McCarthy's *Blood Meridian*. That brief catalog would be achingly incomplete without *The Scarlet Letter,* a permanent center of our imaginative consciousness.

Biography of
Nathaniel Hawthorne

"There is evil in every human heart," wrote Nathaniel Hawthorne in the notebooks in which he recorded his experiences and views of the world for so many years. In Hawthorne's greatest works, his somber, mysterious, carefully structured prose analyzes the problem of the sin inherent in the beautiful and terrible world humans have created.

Hawthorne felt that he had been born into a world of gloom and decay in his hometown of Salem, Massachusetts. He was born on July 4, 1804, the son of Elizabeth and Nathaniel Hathorne (he added the "w" to his name as an adult). Hawthorne was always to complain of the oppressive past that haunted Salem, with the memory of its witch trials and stern Puritans looming over the town. This sense of history's oppressive, stifling force runs throughout Hawthorne's works, in which characters must grapple with the pressures of their inheritances. Hawthorne himself felt burdened by the need to justify his career as a writer in the face of these sober judges, and to release himself from the curse of injustice reaching down over the centuries from the over-stern decrees of the Puritans.

In his childhood, Hawthorne read extensively in classic literature, absorbing *The Faery Queene, Pilgrim's Progress,* the works of Shakespeare and Sir Walter Scott, and endless Gothic romances. The sentiments of these works saturate his own works, lending them a sense of self-knowledge and precision and, at their greatest heights, a great insight into human character.

This grounding in literature stood Hawthorne in good stead during his college years at Bowdoin College in Maine, where he joined the Athenean Literary Society and began to write the first of many short stories. His classmates included writer Henry Wadsworth Longfellow and Franklin Pierce, the future president of the United States, who became one of Hawthorne's closest friends.

Although he was a mediocre student who could not be bothered to study any topics that did not catch his eye, the years at Bowdoin had an enormous influence on Hawthorne's career.

From Bowdoin Hawthorne returned to Salem, to the "chamber under the eaves" at his mother's house where he was to spend so many solitary years. From 1825 to 1837 Hawthorne perfected his craft, writing tales and sketches, and generating ideas for novels and poems. During this time he developed the moral universe that would undergird his later works, reading extensively in both classic and contemporary literature and jotting his responses in his omnipresent notebooks. The first product of this time did not bode well for Hawthorne's later success as an author. Although the novel, *Fanshawe,* provides hints of Hawthorne's later strengths, for the most part it is so derivative and reliant on the tropes of the Gothic romance that it is of little interest to modern readers. Hawthorne himself was so disappointed with it that he recalled and burned all copies. Two years after the publication of *Fanshawe,* in 1830, Hawthorne published his first short story, "The Hollow of the Three Hills," in the *Salem Gazette.* Over the next few years he published several sketches, semiautobiographical works, and tales in various magazines but did not receive much critical or popular attention until he published his first collection of short stories, *Twice-Told Tales,* in 1837.

In the same year he published *Twice-Told Tales,* Hawthorne, who was famously taciturn, self-contained, and cool in temperament, fell deeply in love. The woman—Sophia Peabody—was also from Salem, an invalid whose cheerfulness and good temper were unaffected by her illness. She and Hawthorne became secretly engaged, partially because they feared the disapproval of her family, and partially because they enjoyed the delicious spark of their hidden relationship. Hawthorne realized that his meager earnings as a writer would not be enough to support Sophie as well as himself when they married, so he began lobbying for a political appointment. Since his time at Bowdoin he had been an ardent supporter of the Democratic party, the party of his friend Franklin Pierce and his hero Andrew Jackson. Due to his connections in government, he became the official Measurer of Coal and Salt at the Boston Custom House. Although the post paid well, Hawthorne found that the long hours and physical demands kept him from writing, and after two years he realized that he had to find another way of supporting himself.

He spent a year at Brook Farm, an experimental Utopian community based on Transcendentalist and Socialist philosophy, but found that the romance of farming palled quickly. After leaving Brook Farm,

Hawthorne devoted himself once again to writing full-time in the attic of his family's house. In 1842 he and Sophia were married; they moved to the Old Manse in Concord, Massachusetts. Their three years there were the happiest time of Hawthorne's life, as he wrote, spent time with Henry David Thoreau, Margaret Fuller, and other writers, and worked in the garden with Sophia.

Between 1842 and 1846, when he published his second collection of tales, *Mosses from an Old Manse,* Hawthorne worked steadily and published many of his stories in magazines. After a frustrating stint as Surveyor of the Salem Custom House, which he described humorously in the introduction to *The Scarlet Letter,* Hawthorne embarked on the most prolific and successful part of his career.

The Scarlet Letter, Hawthorne's tragic, brilliant tale of passion and retribution, possesses a strength and depth that he was never to achieve in any of his other works. The novel attained immediate public success, both financially and critically. The overwhelming acclaim invigorated Hawthorne and spurred an astonishing amount of great writing. In the next two years he wrote *The House of the Seven Gables, The Blithedale Romance,* and a campaign biography of his friend Franklin Pierce, as well as publishing a collection of tales and two children's books. Even this prodigious output was not enough to support the family, though, and in 1853 he accepted the position of United States Consul to England from President Franklin Pierce

The years in England solved Hawthorne's financial problems and introduced him to the glorious art and culture of Europe, but the time there dealt a fatal blow to his artistic powers. From 1853 until his death in 1864, he wrote only one novel, *The Marble Faun,* and a collection of articles and essays entitled *Our Old Home.* He was frequently ill and deeply distressed by the looming Civil War that threatened to tear the country apart. Despite the presence of his family, Hawthorne had begun to feel a terrible deep sense of loneliness and loss, and an inability to communicate deeply either personally or in his writing. He began work again and again on various novels, only to break off in frustration. By March of 1864 Sophia was frightened by his haggard, weak appearance; the light had gone out of his eyes. On May 18th, while on a journey to Plymouth, New Hampshire, with Franklin Pierce, Hawthorne died in his sleep, leaving a legacy of imagination and perception unmatched in American fiction. ❀

Plot Summary of
The Scarlet Letter

The Scarlet Letter is Hawthorne's greatest work, as well as his first successful piece of long fiction. The sympathy with which he handles Hester's adultery outraged many of the more Puritanical critics of his day, yet it is precisely this delicacy, this investigation into the question of sin and redemption, that draws many readers today. Hawthorne's moral vision is as concerned with the larger society of Puritan New England as it is with the actions of the individual characters. Throughout the story he questions the adequacy of society to judge its members and to impose appropriate penance. In a tale so concerned with retribution, it is significant that the judges of Boston are utterly unable to punish sin in any but the most obvious sinner. Hester must wear the badge of shame on her breast, although her partner, Dimmesdale, receives only adulation because he is able to hide his wrongdoing. Chillingworth, too, evades censure for what is essentially the murder of his patient.

The themes of *The Scarlet Letter* are varied in scope and importance. At one level this is a thoroughly national tale, in which Hawthorne's Puritan ancestors are used to work through contemporary debates about the literary and visual arts, the place of women, and the constitution of human nature. Other themes, such as morality, fate, and free will, are less inherently tied to time and place. Perhaps the most intriguing question Hawthorne asks is about the nature of sin. Was Hester and Dimmesdale's love inherently sinful, or was the love itself a good that was perverted by social values? And if their love was indeed sin, did the transgression act as a sort of "fortunate fall," like the original sin of Adam and Eve, that caused spiritual enlightenment, or did it act to isolate the characters from the social wellsprings of humanity? This question of Original Sin, with Hester as the woman who falls to the passion of the "forbidden fruit," and Dimmesdale as the man seduced out of his intellectual paradise, is certainly one of the most important themes of the book. However, Pearl's close association with Nature, and her eventual happiness, question the final judgment that has traditionally been leveled on Adam and Eve. *The Scarlet Letter* is about the consequences of breaking a moral code, but Hawthorne is not at all certain that these consequences are entirely negative.

The structure of *The Scarlet Letter* focuses the reader's attention on different aspects of Puritan society, thus providing varying viewpoints on the central action. In the first eight chapters the action is driven by the community; in chapters nine through twelve Chillingworth drives the plot; Hester is responsible for chapters thirteen through twenty; and Dimmesdale is the center of the final chapters. This sectional structure is further developed by three scenes focused on the scaffold in the center of Boston. The story opens with Hester on the scaffold and ends with Dimmesdale's confession on the same scaffold. In the center of the novel the two stand on the pillory with their child, Pearl. This progression illustrates the movement from isolated true penance, to isolated false penance, to voluntary punishment. The novel as a whole follows this falling and rising pattern, with the center of the novel presenting a scene of total darkness. Chillingworth's power is unshakable, Hester utterly bereft of sympathy, Dimmesdale falling fatally ill, and Pearl an uncontrollable and somewhat frightening force. In the second half, however, these relationships reverse, as Hester and Dimmesdale come to ever more self-knowledge and Chillingworth's hold over them is broken.

Hawthorne prefaces his story with a humorous anecdote about his time as Surveyor of the Salem Custom House, surrounded by old men and time-servers. He tells of the fictional "discovery" of a manuscript telling the tale of Hester Prynne, which leads to a discussion of the goals and difficulties that beset a writer of fiction. The essay also sets the tone for his larger investigation of Puritan hypocrisy and judgment.

The story proper begins as Hester Prynne is led out of the Boston jail to the scaffold. A beautiful young woman, she traveled to the New World ahead of her elderly husband, who was captured by Indians upon his arrival and is presumed dead. Left alone, Hester gave in to her passion for the young minister of the colony, Arthur Dimmesdale, and when her adulterous pregnancy was discovered the elders of the colony locked her away. Due to her youth, however, they decided not to kill her or brand her on the forehead, two common punishments for sexual freedom. Instead, they condemn her to stand on the scaffold for three hours to be stared at by the crowd, and then wear a scarlet "A," for adultery, sewn to her clothes for the rest of her life. Hester refuses to name the father of her child, who is now three months old, even when the religious leaders, including Dimmesdale, press her to share her punishment. Hawthorne, too, does not reveal the identity of Pearl's father until late in the novel, which heightens the reader's suspense.

As she stands on the scaffold, clutching little Pearl to her breast and burning with shame, Hester sees her husband standing in the crowd staring at her malevolently. After Hester returns to the jail, she is terrified to see that he has followed her in the guise of a physician, and means to give medicine to her and Pearl. She worries that he means to poison her for her infidelity, but he is determined on a much more subtle and long-lasting revenge, including discovery and punishment of her lover.

After being released from prison, Hester and Pearl go to live in a small cottage on the outskirts of town. She is an object lesson in shame for the rest of the villagers, who scorn her as a fallen woman. Despite their sneers, however, Hester cares for the sick and poor of the town, selflessly giving herself in an effort to redeem her sin. She supports herself and Pearl by her beautiful and artistic needlework, which is greatly in demand among the very people who spurn her. Pearl develops into a strange and fanciful child, whose passionate spirits and violent outbursts of temper set her apart from the other children. She is a constant reminder to Hester of both love and shame, her "happiness and her torture"; in short, the embodiment of the scarlet letter itself.

Meanwhile Roger Chillingworth, Hester's husband, has become the confidante and personal physician of the Reverend Dimmesdale. Burdened with his secret guilt, Dimmesdale's health has become ever more sickly and weak, while his preaching has continued to grow in power and brilliance. Chillingworth acts as a sort of diabolical therapist, digging deep into Dimmesdale's soul for the purpose of ferreting out his secrets and torturing him ruthlessly.

Under the combined torment of Chillingworth's dark insinuations and the adulation of his congregation, which regards him as a sort of saint, Dimmesdale resorts to the hidden penance of sleepless vigils and self-flagellation, but is unable to free himself of his guilt. Finally, in the dead of night he creeps out to the scaffold to stand in a parody of Hester's public shame. She, returning from the death-bed of the Governor, comes accompanied by Pearl to stand with him on the pillory. Just then a strange apparition appears in the sky, a glowing meteor in the shape of an A that sheds its sullen, red light over the three figures. By its light Pearl points at Chillingworth, who stands in the shadows watching them. This episode of Gothic horror forms the pivot of the novel, a mockery of confession in which the characters are utterly isolated from their society.

Hester, whose perceptiveness is much greater than that of Dimmesdale, is well aware that Chillingworth is slowly killing the minister. She confronts her erstwhile husband one day at the sea-shore, asking, "Hast thou not tortured him enough? Has he not paid thee all?" Chillingworth admits that he has become a fiend in his pursuit of Dimmesdale, but refuses to allow Hester to expose the young man's guilt, which would free him from his hell of private guilt and shame. He claims that Dimmesdale cannot be purged of guilt anymore than Chillingworth can be freed of his evil nature, that all events are driven by fate.

Hester next resolves to reveal the truth of Chillingworth's character to Dimmesdale himself. She meets him in the forest, far from the constraints of society and Chillingworth's dark science. During her many years of solitude, Hester had learned to look on human institutions as an outsider would, a view that Hawthorne views as strong but misguided. She urges the minister to flee to Europe and offers to accompany him with Pearl. Filled with joy, he agrees, and Hester tears the scarlet letter from her dress and flings it down on the ground. Pearl, however, breaks into an outburst of passion and forces her mother to take up the emblem once again. In this she acts much as Chillingworth does on Dimmesdale, compelling her mother to confront her guilt. The three leave the woods having agreed to flee after Dimmesdale preaches the Election Day sermon, the culmination of a minister's career.

Freed from his oppressive sense of isolation and shame, and immune to Chillingworth's tortures, Dimmesdale becomes giddily excited over the next few days. He has fantasies of whispering heretical arguments to his most godly parishioners, performing wild, wicked deeds, and seducing young women. These impulses clearly suggest Hawthorne's disapproval of the notion of escape rather than penance as a response to sin.

On the day of the Election, Dimmesdale's sermon is a triumph, full of passion and pathos. As he leaves the church, "he stood on the very proudest eminence of superiority," while Hester "was standing beside the scaffold of the pillory, with the scarlet letter still burning on her breast." The contrast serves neatly to underline the discrepancy between appearance and reality.

When the procession exiting the church passes the scaffold, Dimmesdale, now pale and shaking with a terrible sickness, pauses and calls Hester and Pearl to him. Chillingworth attempts to hold him back, but the minister forces his way up the stairs. Standing with his lover and child, Dimmesdale confesses his guilt to the astonished throng, saying that Hester's scarlet letter is but the physical show of the one he bears on his own breast. He tears his shirt open to reveal what may or may not be a letter imprinted on his flesh. Kissing Hester and Pearl, and praising God's mercy, Dimmesdale dies.

Soon after Dimmesdale's death Chillingworth also dies, leaving extensive estates in England and America to Pearl. She and her mother go to live abroad, until years later Hester returns alone to live once again in her isolated cottage. She voluntarily dons the scarlet letter, yet her selfless behavior and care for others transforms the stigma into a sign of her angelic, artistic nature, rather than any brand of sin. ❀

List of Characters in
The Scarlet Letter

It is **Hester Prynne's** beauty, strength, and passion that lend *The Scarlet Letter* so much of its power. She is a young woman, born in England and transported to Massachusetts colony to be with her grim,
elderly husband, who soon vanishes and leaves her alone. Throughout
the tale, Hester bears her sorrows with a saintly fortitude, ministering
to the sick and poor of the town in an echo of Dimmesdale's work, and
an effort to make up for what she has done. Hester is also a wonderful
seamstress, and her creativity and artistry, linked to her passionate nature, stand in opposition to the dry scholarship of the central male
characters and Puritan leaders. She embodies the American dream of
self-reliance, freedom, and individualism, and in many ways serves as
the novel's center. The bleakness of the punishment she suffers for
these strengths, including her own sense of shame and guilt, raises her
to the position of the tragic heroine.

    Arthur Dimmesdale is the young Puritan minister of Boston, fa-
mous in the colony for his physical attractiveness and holy demeanor,
as well as for the power and persuasiveness of his sermons. However,
Dimmesdale's surface hides the hypocrisy of his relationship with
Hester, and his inability to confess to either his congregation or God.
Throughout the novel he becomes ever more successful in the eyes of
his followers, yet more and more physically ill due to his inner torment
and corruption. He confesses finally when he is at the height of his
reputation, on the day that he gives the Election Sermon. He dies at
the moment of his confession, unsure of his redemption and unable
to bear the torture of his sin. Dimmesdale's characterization is filled
with irony: the irony of the corrupt man responsible for the moral
well-being of his flock, the irony of deepest guilt and confession revealed only at a moment of triumph, the irony of a weak man praised
by society in contrast to the strong woman who is abandoned by it.

    Hester's young daughter **Pearl** has often been critiqued as being
more of a symbol than a truly human character. Dressed by her
mother in brightly ornamented red clothes, Pearl is the scarlet letter
made alive, an "elfin" child who both reinforces her mother's guilt and
helps her to transform sin into love. By the end of the story, Pearl has

become one of the richest heiresses in New England, and presumably an accepted member of society, thus healing the rift caused by her parents' transgression. Hawthorne stresses Pearl's unnaturalness: her storms of temper at the townspeople, her mocking spirit, and her frequently diabolic behavior. Because she is a young child, Pearl is herself guiltless, and this innocence combines with the inherent sinfulness of her birth to make her seem more a child of nature and moral wilderness than of society. She is the symbol of nature, of Hester and Dimmesdale's sin, of the human tainted by original sin, and of the possibility of regeneration in even the most wild heart.

Roger Chillingworth is Hester's first husband, who takes his new name to distance himself from her sin. Much older than she, he filled his life with the study of alchemy and other arcane arts, locking himself away from human society until his marriage. When he arrived in the New World, traveling some time after Hester's voyage, he was captured by an Indian tribe, from whom he learned the skills of a physician. He uses these skills to become close to Dimmesdale, keeping the man's body alive while constantly tormenting his soul with subtle psychological pressure. Chillingworth's perverse character is symbolized both by his "cold" name and by his bodily deformity; he is a hunchback. He comes to symbolize the worst of the Puritan community, its intolerance and utter inability to allow others to live as individuals. His vindictiveness, obsessive anger, and lack of human compassion make his guilt as great as that of the two lovers, and in the end Chillingworth has become virtually a servant of the devil, if not a symbol of Satan himself. ❀

Critical Views of
The Scarlet Letter

ANTHONY TROLLOPE ON SATIRE AND SYMPATHY

[Anthony Trollope (1815–1882) is most famous for his novels, especially the gently comic Barchester series. He also wrote many travel books, short stories, plays, and biographies of famous men such as Thackeray, Cicero, and Lord Palmerston. Here he discusses the impact of satire and sympathy in *The Scarlet Letter.*]

It is so terrible in its pictures of diseased human nature as to produce most questionable delight. The reader's interest never flags for a moment. There is nothing of episode or digression. The author is always telling his one story with a concentration of energy which, as we can understand, must have made it impossible for him to deviate. The reader will certainly go on with it to the end very quickly, entranced, excited, shuddering, and at times almost wretched. His consolation will be that he too has been able to see into these black deeps of the human heart. The story is one of jealousy,—of love and jealousy,—in which love is allowed but little scope, but full play is given to the hatred which can spring from injured love. ⟨ . . . ⟩

He seems hardly to have wished that we should sympathize even with her; or, at any rate, he has not bid us in so many words to do so, as is common with authors. Of course, he has wished it. He has intended that the reader's heart should run over with ruth for the undeserved fate of that wretched woman. And it does. She is pure as undriven snow. We know that at some time far back she loved and sinned, but it was done when we did not know her. We are not told so, but come to understand, by the wonderful power of the writer in conveying that which he never tells, that there has been no taint of foulness in her love, though there has been deep sin. He never even tells us why that letter A has been used, though the abominable word is burning in our ears from first to last. We merely see her with her child, bearing her lot with patience, seeking for no comfort, doing what good she can in her humble solitude by the work of her hands, pointed at from all by the finger of scorn, but the purest, the cleanest, the fairest also among women. She never dreams of supposing that she ought not to be regarded as vile, while the reader's heart glows with a longing to take her soft hand and lead her into some pleasant place where the world shall be pleasant and honest and kind to her. I can fancy a reader so loving the image of Hester Prynne as to find himself on the verge of treachery to the real Hester of flesh and blood who may have a claim upon him. Sympathy can not go beyond that; and yet the author deals with her in a spirit of assumed hardness; almost as though he assented to the judgment and the manner in which it was carried out. In this, however, there is a streak of that satire with which Hawthorne always speaks of the peculiar institutions of his own country. The worthy magistrates of Massachusetts are under his lash throughout the story, and so is the virtue of her citizens and the chastity of her matrons, which can take delight in the open shame of a woman whose sin has been discovered. Indeed, there is never a page written by Hawthorne not tinged by satire.

The fourth character is that of the child, Pearl. Here the author has, I think, given way to a temptation, and in doing so has not increased the power of his story. The temptation was, that Pearl should add a picturesque element by being an elf and also a charming child. Elf she is, but, being so, is incongruous with all else in the story, in which, unhuman as it is, there is nothing of the ghost-like, nothing of the unnatural. The old man becomes a fiend, so to say, during the process of the tale; but he is a man-fiend. And Hester becomes sublimated almost to divine purity; but she is still simply a woman. The minister is tortured beyond the power of human endurance; but neither do his sufferings nor his failure of strength adequate to support them come to him from any miraculous agency. But Pearl is miraculous,—speaking, acting, and thinking like an elf,—and is therefore, I think, a drawback rather than an aid. The desolation of the woman, too, would have been more perfect without the child. It seems as though the author's heart had not been hard enough to make her live alone;— as sometimes when you punish a child you can not drive from your face that gleam of love which shoots across your frown and mars its salutary effect.

—Anthony Trollope, "The Genius of Nathaniel Hawthorne," *The North American Review* 129 (1879): pp. 208, 210–211.

[Henry James (1843–1916) was an American literary critic and master of fiction writing. His best-known works include *The Portrait of a Lady, The Bostonians, The Wings of the Dove,* and *Daisy Miller.* He is also known for his short stories, such as "The Turn of the Screw," and his plays. In both his criticism and fiction James focused on the conflict within cultures and social classes, the relationship of the artist to his art, and the role of women. In this selection he discusses some of the elements that make *The Scarlet Letter* a great novel.]

⟨T⟩he publication of *The Scarlet Letter* was in the United States a literary event of the first importance. The book was the finest piece of imaginative writing yet put forth in the country. There was a consciousness of this in the welcome that was given it—a satisfaction in the idea of America having produced a novel that belonged to literature, and to the forefront of it. Something might at last be sent to Europe as exquisite in quality as anything that had been received, and the best of it was that the thing was absolutely American; it belonged to the soil, to the air; it came out of the very heart of New England.

It is beautiful, admirable, extraordinary; it has in the highest degree that merit which I have spoken of as the mark of Hawthorne's best things—an indefinable purity and lightness of conception, a quality which in a work of art affects one in the same way as the absence of grossness does in a human being. His fancy, as I just now said, had evidently brooded over the subject for a long time; the situation to be represented had disclosed itself to him in all its phases. When I say in all its phases, the sentence demands modification; for it is to be remembered that if Hawthorne laid his hand upon the well-worn theme, upon the familiar combination of the wife, the lover, and the husband, it was after all but to one period of the history of these three persons that he attached himself. The situation is the situation after the woman's fault has been committed, and the current of expiation and repentance has set in. In spite of the relation between Hester Prynne and Arthur Dimmesdale, no story of love was surely ever less of a "love story." To Hawthorne's imagination the fact that these two persons had loved each other too well was of an interest comparatively vulgar; what appealed to him was the idea of their moral situation in the long years that were to follow. The story indeed is in a secondary degree that of Hester Prynne; she becomes, really, after the first scene, an accessory figure; it is not upon her the *dénoûment* depends. It is upon her guilty lover that the author projects most frequently the cold, thin rays of his fitfully-moving lantern, which makes here and there a little luminous circle, on the edge of which hovers the livid and sinister figure of the injured and retributive husband. The story goes on for the most part between the lover and the husband—the tormented young Puritan minister, who carries the secret of his own lapse from pastoral purity locked up beneath an exterior that commends itself to the reverence of his flock, while he sees the softer partner of his guilt standing in the full glare of exposure and humbling herself to the misery of atonement—between this more wretched and pitiable culprit, to whom dishonour would come as a comfort and the pillory as a relief, and the older, keener, wiser man, who, to obtain satisfaction for the wrong he has suffered, devises the infernally ingenious plan of conjoining himself with his wronger, living with him, living upon him, and while he pretends to minister to his hidden ailment and to sympathise with his pain, revels in his unsuspected knowledge of these things and stimulates them by malignant arts.

—Henry James, *Hawthorne* (orig. pub. 1887, London. Reprinted New York: AMS Press, 1968): pp. 111–113.

MARK VAN DOREN ON THE CONFLICT IN HAWTHORNE

[Mark Van Doren (1894–1972) was one of America's most prolific and influential literary critics, authors, and teachers. He was a professor at Columbia University, a winner of the Pulitzer Prize in 1940 for his *Collected Poems,* and a noted author of plays and short stories. His students included Lionel Trilling, Thomas Merton, Jack Kerouac, and Allen Ginsberg, among others. Among his better-known works of criticism are *The Happy Critic and Other Essays, Man's Right to Knowledge and the Free Use Thereof,* and *Invitation to Learning.* In the following excerpt he explores Hawthorne's relationship to Puritan ideology.]

The protagonists of the tale are abstractions, and this time they are neither cold nor empty. Sin, Guilt, Isolation, Pride were not the husks of Hawthorne's thought, they were its deep, warm center, and here for once they operate as personalities, no less divine in their power because they are hidden from sight. The eight satires he had written at the Old Manse, the comprehensive allegories in which he surveyed the contemporary world and found it wanting, had not succeeded even with him. The contemporary world was worth that much of his attention, but he had scattered his fire; had even withheld it, out of a doubt that he knew where he stood. For he was of that world, and much of it he liked. He merely knew that it was wrong when it said with Emerson that self-reliance is a sufficient virtue comprehending all other virtues. "The world has done its best to secure repose without relinquishing evil." The man who could write this could see how little repose was in store for the complacent. He was certain that evil cannot be relinquished—that is, forgotten or wished away. It is the common human heritage, it is the one thing that makes all men, as men, alike. "In Adam's fall we sinned all." And if evil in its extreme forms makes men inhuman by isolating them from their brothers, so does arrogance of spirit. The Transcendental brethren worshipped solitude, which Hawthorne could see only as isolation. His hell, like Dante's, was cold and solitary, a wilderness where nothing blossomed but the will. A warmer world would be one in which men recognized together the ineradicable weakness and corruption of their nature. To him the Puritan world was warmer than his own.

Yet there was much about it that he disliked. It was dismal, it was confined; he would not have had it back. *The Scarlet Letter* in no sense recommends it as a system of thought or a way of life. Hawthorne did not need to believe in Puritanism in order to write a great novel about it. He had only to understand it, which for a man of his time was harder. If it was not impossible for him, the reason is less his experience than his genius, and the fact that something of supreme importance had survived in his lonely thought. He was so alone, so aloof, because he found so few around him whose seriousness equaled his; and by seriousness he meant the real thing, a thing consistent with irony and love, a thing indeed for which comedy might be as suitable an expression as tragedy. If one were serious, one never forgot the eternal importance of every soul, and never doubted that the consequences of deeds, even of impulses, last forever. The Puritans had known this all too well, and their resulting behavior was at times abominable. *The Scarlet Letter* is saying so at the same time that it is revealing a world where tragedy and comedy are possible.

The conflict in Hawthorne of two worlds between which he hung, exposing the fanaticism of one, despising the blandness of the other, is not the least source of *The Scarlet Letter's* power. The book was and is a reminder to modern man, who still talks about his conscience, of where that conscience came from. For Hawthorne it came from a dark world where human injustice was done, but only because men fumbled in their understanding of justice. Justice itself was a form of fate; or, for Hawthorne, so it must seem to any mortal and therefore limited intelligence. To any man "the rickety machine and crazy action of the universe" must appear all but incomprehensible, as at times it did to Hester Prynne.

—Mark Van Doren, *Nathaniel Hawthorne* (New York: William Sloane Associates, 1949): pp. 161–162.

☙

WILLIAM BYSSHE STEIN ON CHILLINGWORTH AND FAUST

[A Fulbright lecturer at the University of Maine and a professor of English at the State University of New York at Binghamton, William Bysshe Stein is an influential scholar of modern American literature and eighteenth-century British literature. He is the author of *The Poetry of Melville's Late Years* and has edited two volumes on Thoreau. In this selection he compares Chillingworth to Faust, the archetypal figure of a search for knowledge at the expense of humanity.]

Chillingworth, it must be remembered, during most of his life dabbles in magical experiments that fall under the jurisdiction of the devil. Yet, unlike Ethan Brand, he is not impelled by the knowledge which he accumulates to break the magnetic chain of humanity; he continually keeps the welfare of mankind in sight. When he marries Hester, he hopes that she will inspire him to greater efforts. She represents his firmest tie to humanity; she epitomizes its sympathy, tenderness, and love. She links him to the deep heart of the universe. Having a profound faith in the integrity of Hester, he sends her to the

New World, intending to follow her after he has arranged his affairs in Europe. Unfortunately, upon arrival he is captured and imprisoned by the Indians. After a lengthy incarceration he is ransomed, and immediately makes his way to the settlement where Hester resides. The first sight that greets his eyes is Hester on the pillory. In the terrible emotional distress that overcomes him, he sees his connection with the magnetic chain of humanity snapped. The grief which floods his heart drives him to a resolution that will, with inexorable finality, exile him from Hester's emotional world. He will, at the propitious moment, sell his soul to the devil, and proclaim his rejection of the brotherhood of man.

To emphasize Chillingworth's essentially heroic stature, Hawthorne sketches him as a Faust, whose prototype we encounter in the dramas. Hester's memories, as she stands on the scaffold, recapture one of her husband's Faustian traits. Her mind's eye dwells on "a pale, thin, scholar-like visage, with eyes dim and bleared by the lamplight that had served them to pore over many ponderous books. Yet those same bleared optics had a strange, penetrating power, when it was their owner's purpose to read the human soul." In the prison-cell scene, as Chillingworth ministers to the ailments of Pearl and Hester, Hawthorne adds another Faustian quality to the scholar's character. Like all Fausts, he has found it necessary to pursue knowledge beyond ordinary limits: and during his captivity with the Indians, he has learned the lore of medicine. Chillingworth, talking to Hester, leaves no doubt about his talents in this study: "My old studies in alchemy . . . and my sojourn . . . among a people well versed in the kindly properties of simples, have made a better physician of me than many that claim the medical degree." Later Hawthorne imputes the old man's extraordinary skill to magic. An aged craftsman in the village declares that Chillingworth was once an associate of the notorious conjurer, Dr. Froman; and other individuals hint that he "had enlarged his medical attainments by joining in the incantations of the savage priests, who were universally acknowledged to be powerful enchanters, often performing seemingly miraculous cures by their skill in the black art." A vulgar rumor prevails that Chillingworth's dark and ugly face betrays his satanic connections. It is said that "the fire in his laboratory had been brought from the lower regions, and was fed with infernal fuel; and so, as might be expected, his visage was getting sooty with the smoke."

At one point in the narrative Hawthorne makes a direct allusion to the scholar's Faustian antecedents: " . . . a rumor gained ground,— and, however absurd, was entertained by some very sensible people,— that Heaven had wrought an absolute miracle, by transporting an eminent Doctor of Physic, from a German university, bodily through the air, and setting him down at the door of Mr. Dimmesdale's study!" Thus Hawthorne succeeds in endowing Chillingworth with the conventional traits of the familiar Fausts. Scholar, alchemist, magician, and physician, he resembles the Faustian hero who moves across the stage in the first scene of Marlowe's and Goethe's dramas.

—William Bysshe Stein, *Hawthorne's Faust: A Study of the Devil Archetype* (Gainesville: University of Florida Press, 1953): pp. 106–108.

⊚

CHARLES CHILD WALCUTT ON THE SYMBOLS OF NATURE

[A professor of English for many years at Queens College and the Graduate School and University Center of the City University of New York, Charles Child Walcutt was the author of *Man's Changing Mask: Modes and Methods of Characterization in Fiction,* and other works on modern and American literature, and was the editor of *Anatomy of Prose.* He is also well known as a pioneer in new methods of teaching basic reading, such as the phonics system. In the essay excerpted below he compares the varied and contradictory readings of *The Scarlet Letter* that have been proposed by the critics, focusing in this selection on the role of nature in the novel.]

The discord among these interpretations of *The Scarlet Letter* may be traced to several causes. First is Hawthorne's symbolism, for his ubiquitous symbols convey meanings different from those communicated by his statements. Nature, for example, operates in the figure of the "wilderness of error" through which Hester is said to wander. Nature asserts itself in Pearl, whose wildness embodies the "freedom of a broken law." Nature originally supplies the impulse of Hester's and Arthur's sin of passion. In these and many other more explicit statements nature acts as a force contrary to the moral law. But nature through other symbols clearly shines upon and approves of Hester and her sin. Beside the prison in Chapter I, the "black flower" of society, grows the rose of love and beauty. Pearl is a rose too, and at the governor's mansion she fortifies this symbolism by crying for a red rose and refusing to be pacified. Pearl, the rose, repeatedly demands that Dimmesdale acknowledge his guilt. Nature shines in Hester's beauty and courage. And the sun of nature, most significantly, shines in blessing upon Hester when, in the forest, she takes off her cap and reveals the rich beauty of her hair. At this point Hester is not acknowledging her sin; rather she is declaring her passion again, her defiance of Puritan rule, and her eagerness to act upon her passion and flee with Dimmesdale to another community in which they can live openly together. This is utter sin, as Hawthorne clearly says, but the force of nature symbols is to draw the reader's sympathy and make him conclude, in spite of the evidence, that the author, too, not only sympathizes with Hester's impulses but also endorses them. What is this evidence? Before the forest walk, Hester lies to Pearl about the scarlet letter. She has "never before been false to the symbol on her bosom," and with this lie a "guardian spirit" forsakes her because "some new evil" has crept into her heart "or some old one had never been expelled." A moment later she speaks to Pearl with unwonted harshness and threatens to shut her in the dark closet. And in the forest meeting which follows, after seeing that Dimmesdale's ruin is the result of her concealment of Chillingworth's identity, it is in defense against his terrible accusations that she declares: "What we did had a consecration of its own." Dimmesdale then says, "Hush, Hester . . . " and "one solemn old tree groaned dolefully to another" over their lost heads, telling their sad story or foreboding "evil to come." After this, in moral darkness they determine to flee, and Hawthorne judges their decision in terms that are not ambiguous. Hester, he writes, had wandered long in a moral wilderness, estranged from human institutions, "criticizing . . . with hardly more reverence than the Indian would feel for the clerical band. . . . Shame, Despair, Solitude! These had been her teachers,—stern and wild ones,—and they had made her strong, but taught her much amiss." These strong words close the paragraph in which Hester is evaluated at the moment of her great choice. ⟨ . . . ⟩

The flood of sunshine that bathes Hester's uncovered hair for a moment does not utter a full benediction on her sin, nor does it express the author's final comment on her moral state. But the reader whose heart inclines that way reacts to the bright nature symbol in the middle of this moral gloom and concludes that it expresses that novel's romantic meaning.

—Charles Child Walcutt, "'The Scarlet Letter' and Its Modern Critics," *Nineteenth-Century Fiction* 7, no. 4 (March 1953): pp. 261–263.

⊚

ROY R. MALE ON PEARL AND CHILLINGWORTH AS SYMBOLS

[A professor of English at the University of Oklahoma, Roy R. Male was a Ford Foundation Fellow in 1954. He is the author of *American Literary Masters, Readings and Writings, Money Talks: Language and Lucre in American Fiction,* and other criticism. In this selection he explores Roger Chillingworth's symbolic value.]

As an abstraction, Pearl is inflexible and inexorable. She has a "hard, metallic lustre" that needs grief to melt it and make her human. Both character and type, both natural and preternatural, she is in time and outside of it. She watches her reflection in the forest brook, the stream of time; a little later we are informed that "the soul beheld its features in the mirror of the passing moment." As a growing child, Pearl serves as an index to the passage of time in the narrative; as a symbol, she indicates to Hester and Arthur that truth cannot be perceived outside its temporal context.

These generations will derive further support when we see Pearl in relation to the two major characters. Meanwhile, having established as a working hypothesis at least that Pearl signifies truth and grace, we may turn to Roger Chillingworth. He has always been recognized as a personification, but it will not suffice to see him simply as evil incarnate. "Under the appellation of Roger Chillingworth . . . was hidden under another name," and the name is not only Prynne—it is Guilt. Hawthorne's portrayal of Chillingworth illustrates how beautifully his imagination could weld the abstract to the concrete. For the physician is interesting in his own right as an alchemist-psychiatrist manqué, who tries to solve the riddle of man's existence by logical or psychological analysis.

As a symbol of guilt, Chillingworth is a leech, draining his patient of nerve, will, and physical energy. But, as the whole book demonstrates, he is also the healer. Only by knowing him, confronting him face to face, is moral growth possible. Not that moral growth is guaranteed or that having this unwelcome guest is "fortunate"—it is simply inevitable in human existence. "The breach which guilt has once made into the human soul is never in this mortal state repaired. It may be watched and guarded; so that the enemy shall not force his way again *into the citadel*, and might even, in his subsequent assaults, select some other avenue, in preference to that where he had formerly succeeded. But there is still *the ruined wall.*" The italicized phrases remove all doubt of Chillingworth's identity. As guilt he invades the dwelling place, which, as we know, is customarily a symbol for the heart in Hawthorne's fiction. "My home," he tells Hester, "is where thou art and where he [the minister] is." Early in the book Chillingworth appears from nowhere to confront Hester in the prison cell of her heart; by the middle of the book he has insinuated himself into Dimmesdale's abode. "A deformed old figure, with a face that haunted men's memories longer than they liked," he gradually shrivels as Hester and Dimmesdale come closer to full recognition of him.

—Roy R. Male, *Hawthorne's Tragic Vision* (Austin: University of Texas Press, 1957): pp. 95–97.

⊛

Richard Harter Fogle on the Four States of Being

[Richard Harter Fogle has taught English at Tulane University and the University of North Carolina at Chapel Hill. He is the author of *The Imagery of Keats and Shelley* and *Hawthorne's Imagery*, as well as other volumes on American and romantic writing. In this section, he discusses the four states of being in *The Scarlet Letter*, and shows how the combination of the four lends the novel its sense of balance and complexity.]

There are four states of being in Hawthorne: one subhuman, two human, and one superhuman. The first is Nature, which comes to our attention in *The Scarlet Letter* twice. It appears first in the opening chapter, in the wild rosebush which stands outside the blackbrowed Puritan jail. ⟨. . .⟩ The second entrance of Nature comes in the forest scene, where it sympathizes with the forlorn lovers and gives them hope. "Such was the sympathy of Nature—that wild, heathen Nature of the forest, never subjugated by human law, nor illuminated by higher truth. . . . " The sentence epitomizes both the virtues of Nature and its inadequacy. In itself good, Nature is not a sufficient support for human beings.

The human levels are represented by Hawthorne's distinction between Heart and Head. The heart is closer to nature, the head to the supernatural. The heart may err by lapsing into nature, which means, since it has not the innocence of nature, into corruption. The danger of the head lies in the opposite direction. It aspires to be superhuman, and is likely to dehumanize itself in the attempt by violating the human limit. Dimmesdale, despite his considerable intellect, is predominantly a heart character, and it is through the heart that sin has assailed him, in a burst of passion which overpowered both religion and reason. The demoniac Chillingworth is of the head, a cold experimenter and thinker. It is fully representative of Hawthorne's general emphasis that Chillingworth's spiritual ruin is complete. Hester Prynne is a combination of head and heart, with a preponderance of head. Her original sin is of passion, but its consequences expose her to the danger of absolute mental isolation. The centrifugal urge of the intellect is counteracted in her by her duty to her daughter Pearl, the product of the sin, and by her latent love for Dimmesdale. Pearl herself is a creature of nature, most at home in the wild forest: " . . . the mother-forest, and these wild things which it nourished, all recognized a kindred witness in the human child." She is made human by Dimmesdale's confession and death: "The great scene of grief, in which the wild infant bore a part, has developed all her sympathies. . . . "

The fourth level, the superhuman or heavenly, will perhaps merely be confused by elaborate definition. It is the sphere of absolute insight, justice, and mercy. Few of Hawthorne's tales and romances can be adequately considered without taking it into account. As Mark Van Doren has recently emphasized, it is well to remember Hawthorne's belief in immortality. It is because of the very presence of the superhuman in Hawthorne's thinking that the destinies of his chief characters are finally veiled in ambiguity. He respects them as he would have respected any real person by refusing to pass the last judgment, by leaving a residue of mysterious individuality untouched. The whole truth is not for a fellow human to declare.

These four states are not mutually exclusive. ⟨. . .⟩ In some respects the highest and the lowest of these levels are most closely akin, as if their relationship were as points of a circle. The innocence of nature is like the innocence of heaven. It is at times, when compared to the human, like the Garden before the serpent, like heaven free of the taint of evil. Like infancy, however, nature is a stage which man must pass through, whereas his destination is heaven. The juxtaposition of highest and lowest nevertheless involves difficulties, when perfect goodness seems equivalent to mere deprivation and virtue seems less a matter of choosing than of being untempted.

—Richard Harter Fogle, *Hawthorne's Fiction: The Light and the Dark* (Norman: University of Oklahoma Press, 1964): pp. 135–138.

⟨ঌ⟩

Frederick C. Crews on Dimmesdale's Libido

[Frederick C. Crews is a professor of English at the University of California, Berkeley. The editor of *Great Short Works of Nathaniel Hawthorne, Psychoanalysis and the Literary Process,* and the *Random House Handbook,* Frederick Crews's early criticism was strongly influenced by the work of Sigmund Freud. He later repudiated his belief in Freud in such works as *Out of My System: Psychoanalysis, Ideology and Critical Method,* and *Skeptical Engagements.* The excerpt below, taken from Crews's early works, examines Arthur Dimmesdale's behavior in terms of Freud's theories of libido and repression.]

⟨Dimmesdale's⟩ nervousness, his mental exhaustion, and his compulsive gesture of placing his hand on his heart reveal a state that we would now call neurotic inhibition. His lack of energy for any of the outward demands of life indicates how all-absorbing is his internal trouble, and the stigma on his chest, though a rather crass piece of symbolism on Hawthorne's part, must also be interpreted psychosomatically. Nor can we avoid observing that Dimmesdale shows the neurotic's reluctance to give up his symptoms. How else can we account for his obtuseness in not having recognized Chillingworth's character? "I might have known it!" he murmurs when Hester forces the revelation upon him. "I did know it! Was not the secret told me in the natural recoil of my heart, at the first sight of him, and as often as I have seen him since? Why did I not understand?" The answer, hidden from Dimmesdale's surface reasoning, is that his relationship with Chillingworth, taken together with the change in mental economy that has accompanied it, has offered perverse satisfactions which he is even now powerless to renounce. Hester, whose will is relatively independent and strong, is the one who makes the decision to break with the past.

We can understand the nature of Dimmesdale's illness by defining the state of mind that has possessed him for seven years. It is of course his concealed act of adultery that lies at the bottom of his self-torment. But why does he lack the courage to make his humiliation public? Dimmesdale himself offers us the clue in a cry of agony: "Of penance I have had enough! Of penitence there has been none! Else, I should long ago have thrown off these garments of mock holiness, and have shown myself to mankind as they will see me at the judgment-seat." The plain meaning of this outburst is that Dimmesdale has never surmounted the libidinal urge that produced his sin. His "penance," including self-flagellation and the more refined torment of submitting to Chillingworth's influence, has failed to purify him because it has been unaccompanied by the feeling of penitence, the resolution to sin no more. ⟨ . . . ⟩

This conclusion may seem less paradoxical if we bear in mind a distinction between remorse and true repentance. In both states the sinful act is condemned morally, but in strict repentance the soul abandons the sin and turns to holier thoughts. Remorse of Dimmesdale's type, on the other hand, is attached to a continual re-enacting of the sin in fantasy and hence a continual renewal of the need for self-punishment. Roger Chillingworth, the psychoanalyst *manqué*, understands the process perfectly: "the fear, the remorse, the agony, the ineffectual repentance, the backward rush of sinful thoughts, expelled in vain!" As Hawthorne explains, Dimmesdale's cowardice is the "sister and closely linked companion" of his remorse.

Thus Dimmesdale is helpless to reform himself at this stage because the passional side of his nature has found an outlet, albeit a self-destructive one, in his present miserable situation. The original sexual desire has been granted recognition *on the condition of being punished,* and the punishment itself is a form of gratification. Not only the overt masochism of fasts, vigils, and self-scourging (the last of these makes him laugh, by the way), but also Dimmesdale's emaciation and weariness attest to the spending of his energy against himself. It is important to recognize that this is the same energy previously devoted to passion for Hester. We do not exaggerate the facts of the romance in saying that the question of Dimmesdale's fate, for all its religious decoration, amounts essentially to the question of what use is to be made of his libido.

—Frederick C. Crews, *The Sins of the Fathers: Hawthorne's Psychological Themes* (New York: Oxford University Press, 1966): pp. 140–142.

ⓑ

Michael J. Colacurcio on Hester Prynne and Anne Hutchinson

[After teaching American literature and intellectual history at Cornell University for many years, Michael Colacurcio is now a professor at the University of California at Los Angeles. He acted as the technical consultant to the *Scarlet Letter* project for WGBH, Boston, and edited a collection of essays on *The Scarlet Letter.* He is also the author of two volumes on early American literature: *Province of Piety* and *Doctrine and Difference.* In the following extract he compares Hester Prynne to the famous religious leader Anne Hutchinson (spelled here Ann).]

In the first brief chapter of *The Scarlet Letter,* the narrator pays almost as much attention to a rose bush as he does to the appearance and moral significance of Puritan America's first prison. That "wild rose-bush, covered, in this month of June, with its delicate gems," contrasts with the "burdock, pig-weed, apple-peru" and other "unsightly vegetation"; yet all flourish together in the same "congenial" soil which has so early brought forth "the black flower of civilized society, a prison." And thus early are we introduced to the book's extremely complicated view of the natural and the social. Moreover, as the rose bush seems to offer Nature's sympathy to society's criminal, it becomes essentially associated with Hester Prynne, almost as *her* symbol. Accordingly, criticism has been lavish in its own attention to that rose bush: it has, out of perfect soundness of instinct, been made the starting point of more than one excellent reading of *The Scarlet Letter;* indeed the explication of this image and symbol is one of the triumphs of the "new" Hawthorne criticism.

But if the "natural" and internal associations of this rose bush have been successfully elaborated, its external and "historic" implications have been largely ignored. And yet not for any fault of the narrator. This rose bush "has been kept alive in history," he assures us; and it may even be, as "there is fair authority for believing," that "it had sprung up under the footsteps of the sainted Ann Hutchinson, as she entered the prison-door." ⟨ . . . ⟩

Like Ann Hutchinson, Hester Prynne is an extraordinary woman who falls afoul of a theocratic and male-dominated society; and the problems which cause them to be singled out for exemplary punishment both begin in a special sort of relationship with a pastor who is one of the acknowledged intellectual and spiritual leaders of that society. No overt sexual irregularity seems to have been associated with Mrs. Hutchinson's denial that converted saints were under the moral law, but (as we shall see later) no one could read what seventeenth-century Puritan observers said about the "seductiveness" of her doctrines without sensing sexual implications everywhere. Evidently such implications were not lost on Hawthorne. Further, though with increasing complications, both of these remarkable and troublesome women have careers as nurses and counsellors to other women: Ann Hutchinson begins her prophetic career this way, whereas Hester Prynne moves in this direction as a result of her punishment. And most significantly—if most problematically—both make positive pronouncements about the inapplicability of what the majority of their contemporaries take to be inviolable moral law.

To be sure, it takes Hester Prynne some time to catch up with Ann Hutchinson; but when Hawthorne says of Hester, in the full tide of her later speculative freedom, that "the world's law was no law to her mind", we may well suspect that he intends some conscious pun on the literal meaning of "antinomianism." If Hester's problems begin with sex more literally than do Ann Hutchinson's, her thinking eventually ranges far outward from that domestic subject. In some way, and for complicated reasons that need to be examined, Hester Prynne and sex are associated in Hawthorne's mind with Ann Hutchinson and spiritual freedom. ⟨ . . . ⟩ᐧ

Waiving the problem of vehicle and tenor, we may validly conclude that in *The Scarlet Letter* "the woman's" discovery of an authentic, valid, and not shameful sexual nature is not unlike the Self's discovery of its own interior, "spiritual" sanction. The *donnée* of Hawthorne's romance is such that Hester discovers both together, and each reinforces the other.

—Michael J. Colacurcio, "Footsteps of Ann Hutchinson: The Context of *The Scarlet Letter*," *ELH* 39, no. 3 (September 1972): pp. 459, 461–462, 485.

⊗

SHERIDAN BAKER ON DIMMESDALE'S SCARLET A

[A professor of English at the University of Michigan, Sheridan Baker is a Fellow of the Rockefeller Foundation in Bellagio, Italy. He has taught at the University of Nagoya, Japan, as a Fulbright lecturer. He is the author of *The Practical Stylist, The Complete Stylist and Handbook,* and *Ernest Hemingway: An Introduction and Interpretation,* as well as being the co-editor of *The Harper Handbook of Literature.* In this selection he discusses the ambiguity surrounding the presence of a scarlet A on the chest of the Reverend Arthur Dimmesdale.]

The *origin* of the letter, not its actuality, produces the several theories, among which, Hawthorne says, the reader may choose. The whole point of this last chapter is how witnesses will rationalize, and even rationalize away, the evidence before their eyes. Our omniscient narrator, however obliquely, has told us unmistakably that Dimmesdale's breast bore a visible and actual *A,* a psychosomatic rash, the sign of the painful adulterous *A* he has hidden in his heart. Chillingworth has seen it (though we don't see what he sees), bursting into diabolical ecstasy at this confirmation of his suspicions, when he bares the sleeping and exhausted Dimmesdale's breast. When Hawthorne entitles his final scaffold chapter "The Revelation of the Scarlet Letter," he gives us omniscient evidence straight: not "*a* Scarlet Letter" nor "*Another* Scarlet Letter" nor "a confused revelation of what some witnesses and future critics may theorize was or was not a scarlet letter," but "*the*

Scarlet Letter," the real one that book has been about, that of the hidden hypocritical guilt rather than the one emblazoned on Hester, which we had assumed from the first and cannot cease from assuming. Look again at Dimmesdale's revelation, as he insists that the real letter was not on Hester but on him. God's eye beheld it, as the devil continually fretted it with his burning finger, he says. Hester's is

> "... but the shadow of what he bears on his own breast, and ... even this, his own red stigma, is no more than the type of what has seared his inmost heart.... Behold! ... "

> With a convulsive motion he tore away the ministerial band from before his breast. It was revealed! But it were irreverent to describe the revelation.

The letter is there, and no mistake, Dimmesdale has described it for us sufficiently, before Hawthorne turns away to describe the consequences of its revelation. The crowd is horror-stricken.

The last chapter then records the curiosities of human rationalization. When, "After many days," people have had enough time to get their thoughts together, most of them theorizing about how the devil the letter got there, and a few—"It is singular"—who "professed never once to have removed their eyes" from Dimmesdale, "even denying any mark whatsoever." Hawthorne goes on to wonder at this exercise of upholding a man's character, even "when proofs clear as the midday sunshine on the scarlet letter, establish him a false and sin-stained creature of dust." Hawthorne might also have liked to wonder at those critics who continue to assert that Dimmesdale's breast may or may not have been emblazoned with a painful red *A*, reader's choice.

—Sheridan Baker, "Hawthorne's Evidence," *Philological Quarterly* 61, no. 4 (Fall 1982): pp. 481–482.

Ⓢ

TERENCE MARTIN ON DIMMESDALE'S CHARACTER

[Terence Martin is a professor of English at Indiana University and has also taught at universities in France, Germany, Poland, and India. He served on the editorial board of *American Literature,* and has published numerous articles on American artists ranging from Willa Cather and Edgar Allan

Poe to Ken Kesey. His best-known work is *Parables of Possibility: The American Need for Beginnings*. In this excerpt he discusses Dimmesdale's inherent selfishness, an important aspect of a work so concerned with the difference between appearance and reality.]

Dimmesdale clearly suffers from an excess of self. His weakness and suffering throughout most of the romance, as I suggested earlier, have tended to blur for some readers the fact of his pride, which, like his scarlet letter, lies beneath and gives special form to his mask of saintliness. Self-condemnation, self-abnegation, and self-loathing are the stimulants of Dimmesdale's psychic life; they constitute, as well, the price he must pay if he would not abdicate the self reverenced by the public. And that self—formed out of a communal wish to admire a young, pious, and learned minister—he cannot bring himself to renounce. That his private suffering contributes to the public mask of spirituality is a kind of masochistic dividend for him. Weak and proud, false and efficacious, the minister thus stumbles ever deeper and ever more self-consciously into thickets of hypocrisy. Perhaps the most telling example occurs during the forest interview when Dimmesdale inquires of Hester when the ship on which they now plan to sail is scheduled to depart and considers it "most fortunate" that it will not leave for four days. With a posture of reluctance, Hawthorne interprets the minister's thoughts—in order "to hold nothing back from the reader." Dimmesdale considers the departure date "very fortunate" because in three days he is to preach the Election Day sermon, "and, as such an occasion formed an honorable epoch in the life of a New England clergyman, he could not have chanced upon a more suitable mode and time of terminating his professional career. 'At least, they shall say of me,' thought this exemplary man, 'that I leave no public duty unperformed, nor ill performed!'" Hawthorne laments the fact that the minister could be "so miserably deceived": "We have had, and may still have, worse things to tell of him; but none, we apprehend, so pitiably weak; no evidence, at once so slight and irrefragable, of a subtle disease, that had long since begun to eat into the real substance of his character." To wear one face in private and another in public for a considerable period of time, Hawthorne concludes, leaves a man finally "bewildered as to which may be the true."

As the final step in a developing process, Hawthorne has shown us an absolutely stunning doubleness in the minister's character. Having chosen to breathe "the wild, free atmosphere of an unredeemed, unchristianized, lawless region," having undergone a "total change of dynasty and moral code," Dimmesdale reaffirms to himself (he does not mention it to Hester) the importance of the Election Day sermon. He wants to have it both ways, to leave, but to leave with his "public duty" well performed—which is to say, with the congregation marveling at their saintly and inspired minister. Let us note that Dimmesdale's motive here is characteristically secret. No sooner is he converted to Hester's romantic cult than he has an immediate private life outside it which gives him latitude to plan by himself, for himself. The psychological keenness informing Dimmesdale's transformation is of a high order. No matter what "religion" the minister professes, he serves ultimately the interests of one master—himself. Thus, in keeping with the brilliant economy of *The Scarlet Letter,* the moment at which Dimmesdale commits himself consciously to deadly liberating sin becomes the moment at which he secretly wishes to cap his public life with a final burst of eloquence on the most important occasion the Puritan community can offer.

—Terence Martin, *Nathaniel Hawthorne* (Boston: Twayne Publishers, 1983): pp. 122–124.

Plot Summary of
The House of the Seven Gables

Like *The Scarlet Letter, The House of the Seven Gables* investigates the problem of inherited sin, but with a far more hopeful, quietly joyful tone. In it, Hawthorne questions how a cycle of revenge, similar to that found in the Greek myth of the House of Atreus and Shakespeare's *Romeo and Juliet,* can be broken. The novel, or romance as Hawthorne named it, is set in contemporary Salem, a town imbued with a Puritan past of witchcraft, betrayal, and greed. It is this past, with its overlays of aristocracy and inequality, which must be overturned by the modern rise of democracy and pragmatism. Yet the past cannot be dismissed simply, as it is by the footloose Holgrave; it must be healed. The past is symbolized by the House of the Seven Gables, a decaying mansion built on land stolen by an upper-class Puritan, Colonel Pyncheon, from the working-class Matthew Maule. Throughout the years the Pyncheons have built up vast amounts of property and wealth, but their reliance on their social position has made them weak and alienated, unable to cope with daily life. Other themes include the opposition between intellect, symbolized by Holgrave, and imagination, seen in the weak aestheticism of Clifford; we see also the opposition between law and compassion, between appearance and reality, and between psychological isolation and communal existence.

The House of the Seven Gables draws much of its inspiration from the tradition of the Gothic romance, a genre springing from eighteenth-century English literature. Gothic romance is characterized by an overall atmosphere of dread, combining terror with horror and mystery as it emphasizes the mysterious, the supernatural, the despairing man adrift in a dark world. Gothic novels often concern haunted houses, mysterious crimes, and magic, with an evil villain whose dark designs upon an innocent heroine are thwarted at the last minute. Clearly Hawthorne's work is more complicated than such potboilers, strengthened by psychological insight, action that is generally realistic, and subtle levels of symbolism.

The structure of *The House of the Seven Gables* has often been criticized for being fragmentary and disconnected, as though it were more a series of short anecdotes than a coherent narrative. However, this view overlooks the several unifying themes discussed earlier, as well as the gradual building of tone and theme created by the alternation of allegory and action. Throughout the work, Hawthorne moves between long, realistic descriptions of the house and its surroundings and quick bursts of energetic action, using each segment as a discrete building block of the whole. Overall, the novel falls into the shape of an ascending line. The initial darkness and isolation of the characters, each of whom tends more toward light or dark, and past or present, is resolved into an equilibrium in which each can contribute toward a healthy community.

Hawthorne stresses the theme of the past's interaction with the present in the first chapter of the novel. Beginning with a description of the House of the Seven Gables as it stands, dark and decaying, in contemporary Salem, he then describes the boundary dispute that led to the founding of the house. An obscure farmer, Matthew Maule, owned a small house next to a spring of good water on Salem peninsula. The spot was desired by Colonel Pyncheon, a wealthy and respectable Puritan, who claimed to have been given the land some time before. Hawthorne implies that the claim is fictitious, that the Pyncheons' interest in the land springs only from greed and a desire for power. Colonel Pyncheon is able to seize the land only upon the death of Matthew Maule, who is executed for witchcraft at the instigation of the very same Colonel. As Colonel Pyncheon sits on his horse, gazing grimly at the execution, Maule curses him from the scaffold, exclaiming "God will give him blood to drink!"

The curse is carried out when the Colonel dies in his new house of a fit of apoplexy or stroke, sitting dead in his chair with a gush of blood on the ruff of his shirt. His death deprives the Pyncheon family of its greatest hope of power and money: a claim to extensive territories in Maine. A deed of the grant exists, signed by various Indian tribes and governors of the colony, but only the Colonel knows where it is, and his son is too weak to press the claim. Throughout the years, the lost land in Maine will impose "an absurd delusion of family importance" on the Pyncheons, a delusion that weakens them spiritually and keeps them from taking their proper place in a democracy.

The Pyncheons are haunted also by a portrait of the Colonel, glowering down from the wall so "that no good thoughts or purposes could ever spring up and blossom there." Two hundred years later, at the time of the present tale, the Pyncheon family is small and poor, with the single exception of Judge Jaffrey Pyncheon. He is the embodiment of the old Colonel, just as outwardly respectable and inwardly evil as his ancestor. His cousin Hepzibah, living alone in the House of the Seven Gables, has recently decided to open a small store, or cent shop, in the house so that she and her brother Clifford will not have to rely on the Judge's charity. She is distraught at having to engage in commerce, which she thinks is beneath her, but will do anything to make her brother happy. He has recently returned from a thirty-year prison sentence, imposed when Jaffrey framed him for their uncle's death. Hepzibah's embarrassment, her constant nearsighted scowl, and her lack of business acumen make her a terrible shopkeeper, and only the unexpected arrival of her cousin, cheerful Phoebe Pyncheon, keeps the store afloat.

Phoebe's presence also serves to cheer up Clifford, whose spirits have been broken by his term in jail. She cares for the garden and the small, decrepit flock of chickens, both of which symbolize the Pyncheon family in their weakness, illness, and impotence. Phoebe also draws Holgrave, a daguerrotypist who lodges in one of the gables, into the family circle, an act symbolic of reconciliation between the Maule and Pyncheon families.

At one point Holgrave takes Phoebe aside and tells her an eerie story taken from the Pyncheon history. In hopes of recovering the land in Maine, Colonel Pyncheon's grandson, Gervase, entered into a contract with Matthew Maule's grandson, in which Maule would disclose the whereabouts of the missing deed in return for title to the land on which the House of the Seven Gables stood. Maule, however, determined to take his revenge on the family by hypnotizing Gervase's lovely and talented daughter, Alice. With her utterly within his power, Maule attempts to find the deed through magical contact with the spirit of Colonel Pyncheon, but is thwarted by his own ancestors' presence. Maule departs, and soon after the helpless Alice, who is still caught within his spell, wastes away and dies. This story, which is quite unlike the generally realistic main narrative, is virtually a parody of Gothic romance, with its spirits, hypnotic power, and even a haunted portrait of Colonel Pyncheon, which comes alive in a rage upon seeing Gervase's deal to relinquish the House.

While Holgrave, who is actually a descendent of the Maules, is telling the story, Phoebe falls into the same trance that afflicted Alice. Holgrave, however, refuses to become caught in the cycle of the past and releases her with a wave of the hand. It is this ability to turn away from the past that is crucial to Hawthorne and is the central theme of the novel.

In contrast to Holgrave's focus on the present is Judge Jaffrey Pyncheon, who epitomizes all of the family's obsessions and faults. Believing that Clifford knows where the lost deed is to be found, he appears at the house and demands a meeting with his cousin. Despite his terror and weakness, Clifford enters the parlor where Jaffrey waits, only to find the Judge dead in his chair, his blood-covered shirtfront a frightening echo of the Colonel's death. Clifford is so horrified by the discovery that he sweeps his sister up and the two flee away from the house, escaping the town by train. Their flight, on the then excitingly new technology of the train, is their first attempt to escape from the pressures of the house and its past. Clifford is possessed by a hectic energy, unlike his usual artistic lethargy, but Hepzibah feels herself even more alone than she was in her shop. Her brother engages in an agitated discussion with a man on the train, complaining of the dismal and oppressive force that old houses exert on their inhabitants: "The greatest possible stumbling-blocks in the path of human happiness and improvement, are these heaps of bricks, and stones. . . . The soul needs air; a wide sweep and frequent change of it." Soon enough this flush of insight and decisiveness leaves him, and the two trail back to the House of the Seven Gables.

At this point Hawthorne introduces a long, digressive chapter addressed to the corpse of Jaffrey Pyncheon. He lists all of the appointments Jaffrey is missing, emphasizing the gap between temporal power and influence and the mortality of the body. His hypocritical façade of sunny kindness has been stripped away, revealing the darkness and moral lifelessness that have always truly possessed him. The body is discovered by Holgrave and Phoebe, who are shocked into clinging together by the horrible sight. In the face of death, specifically the symbolic death of the worst attributes of the Pyncheon past, they confess their love for each other and become engaged. Hawthorne wraps up the story with a determined cheerfulness, intent on leaving no vestige of darkness. Clifford is so invigorated by the death of his terrifying cousin that he becomes happy and more or less healthy; Hepzibah is able to retreat from the shop; and the entire family moves to their country house with the money left to Phoebe in Jaffrey's will. Even the ominous portrait of Colonel Pyncheon is vanquished, falling to the ground to reveal a secret compartment containing the deed to the Maine land. Bringing the deed into the light, the surviving Pyncheons realize how useless it is, since the land has long been owned and occupied by other people. Free of the pretensions of aristocracy it represents, and with Phoebe married to the descendent of Matthew Maule, the Pyncheon family is ready to leave the House of the Seven Gables and begin anew. ❀

List of Characters in
The House of the Seven Gables

The young, cheerful cousin of Hepzibah and Clifford Pyncheon, **Phoebe Pyncheon** embodies Hawthorne's favorite feminine graces. She is beautiful, self-reliant, and resourceful, eager to help those around her and unacquainted with any touch of evil. Phoebe is also the bright future of the Pyncheon clan, adept at the practical and democratic matters that her aristocratic relatives have scorned. Her father married outside of his social class, another aspect of Phoebe's characterization that promises freedom from the Pyncheon stagnation and pretensions of aristocracy. While early reviewers praised Phoebe for her charming qualities, later readers have found her one-sided sweetness to be cloying, sexist, and overly sentimental. Certainly Phoebe's innocence seems at times overdone, as though she were an Eve who refused even to notice the existence of the serpent. Her excessive cheeriness and inability to confront any darkness or complexity must be balanced out by the influence of her dismal relatives and the restless Holgrave. Phoebe's character is based in many ways on that of Hawthorne's wife, Sophia, whose cheerfulness and good sense he venerated.

Phoebe's elderly cousin, **Hepzibah Pyncheon**, is characterized best by her perpetual scowl and her rusty-black turban. She scowls because she is nearsighted; although her scowling is not due to any ill temper, the residents of Salem are unable to see beneath her surface and laugh at her "irritable" demeanor. This split between appearance and reality is one of the most significant themes of the novel. Hepzibah's turban symbolizes her obsession with the past and its fashions, and her inability to communicate with those around her. She is an eccentric spinster, both pathetic and comical, whose good intentions and genuine sweetness are hampered by her isolation and lack of common sense. Hepzibah's obsession with her gentility is, however, a serious flaw, one that must be countered by her distasteful yet healthy foray into commerce.

Hepzibah's brother, **Clifford Pyncheon**, has just returned from a long imprisonment caused by their cousin Jaffrey Pyncheon. When Jaffrey's uncle died of a heart attack upon finding Jaffrey ransacking his chambers, Jaffrey fixed suspicion for the death on Clifford. The subsequent trial and thirty years in jail have broken Clifford's overly delicate and aesthetic spirits, leaving him a virtual child. Clifford, unlike Holgrave, allows his artistic, poetic sensibilities to render him weak and selfish, incapable of loving his sister because she is not beautiful, and incapable of interacting with the world because he cannot release himself from the dead weight of his ancestors. Many modern critics have seen Clifford as a schizophrenic character, who alternates between excessive energy and utter lethargy. He is obsessed with beauty, but at the same time entirely caught up in the sensual pleasures of eating and drinking. In the end Clifford is shocked out of his arrested development by the discovery of his dead cousin Jaffrey, and his extravagant energy and interest on the train suggest that he may finally be able to move into the future and achieve some sense of completion.

Hepzibah and Clifford's cousin, **Judge Jaffrey Pyncheon**, is the epitome of the split between appearance and reality. Externally he is wealthy, affable, and honorable. As judge, he occupies a position of authority and power in Salem, and is respected by all. However, this façade covers up a selfish, greedy, and heartless man, preoccupied with winning back the family fortunes at any cost. He is a cruel capitalist, a hypocrite, and a thief, all hidden under the image of the responsible father figure. As seen in the eerily revealing daguerreotype, Jaffrey Pyncheon is almost the reincarnation of their ancestor, Colonel Pyncheon, who was suspected of killing Matthew Maule to steal the land for the House of the Seven Gables. Thus Jaffrey serves as the emblem of the negative influence of the past, continuing the rapacity and hard-heartedness of the Puritans. Jaffrey's death at the end of the novel is an inevitable occurrence if Holgrave, Phoebe, and the rest of the Pyncheons are to be free at last of the family curse.

If Jaffrey is the embodiment of the past, **Holgrave** is the very picture of modern young America. Presently a daguerrotypist, he has practiced almost a dozen occupations, wandering about the world unable to settle down in any society. He condemns the past utterly, exclaiming to Phoebe, "Shall we never, never get rid of this Past! It lies upon the Present like a giant's dead body." Hawthorne reveals late in the novel that Holgrave is a descendent of Matthew Maule, the magician killed by Colonel Pyncheon. Holgrave possesses the Maule powers of mesmerism, a form of hypnosis, but uses them for good. He is a lodger in Hepzibah's house, living apart in one of the seven gables until Phoebe's arrival brings him into the world of society. Careless and rootless, Holgrave lives by his own laws, and Hawthorne implicitly critiques the shallowness of his life and philosophy. His transformation from sardonic outsider to home-loving family man is one of the crucial elements of the novel. In many ways Holgrave seems an echo of Hawthorne himself, in his artistic nature, his solitude, and his beliefs about the past. ✿

Critical Views of
The House of the Seven Gables

Lawrence Sargent Hall on Inherited Sin

[Lawrence Sargent Hall received the O. Henry Memorial Award in 1960 and the Faulkner Foundation Award in 1962, both for his fiction. He is also the author of *How Thinking Is Written* and *A Grammar of Literary Criticism*. He teaches at Bowdoin College. In this selection he argues that in *The House of the Seven Gables* Hawthorne used the decay of the Pyncheon family to represent the conflict between aristocracy and democracy in American history.]

The House of Seven Gables constitutes Hawthorne's most forthright use of American democratic philosophy as a basis for a social ethic. The theme of this romance has to do with inherited sin, the sin of aristocratic pretensions against a moral order which, in the judgment of an equalitarian like Hawthorne, calls for a truer and higher evaluation of man. For the inheritance of the Pyncheon family proves to be no more than the antagonism of the old Colonel and his world toward things democratic.

Hawthorne was a shrewd enough student of history to be aware that the Puritan society of New England had been as aristocratic in its way as the feudal society of Europe, with which he was later to have a firsthand acquaintance. He saw clearly the sharp cleavage that existed then between the various members of the social group. The servants who stood inside the entrance to the House of the Seven Gables directing one class of people to the parlor and the other to the kitchen preside likewise over the social distinctions of the whole story, separating the Pyncheons from the Maules and gentility from democracy until the very end. It is Hawthorne's symbolism at its best.

By rendering the Pyncheon claim to such territory a snare and a delusion, Hawthorne signified the baselessness of the pretensions of gentility and its gradual absorption in the morally inevitable progress of society toward democracy.

But the Pyncheon family itself (like the illusion of property upon which still depended much of the pride that was the mainstay of their spirit) gradually became more and more attenuated as the falseness of their position was made clearer by the great movement of society toward the equalitarian ideal. In fact, by the time the story proper opens, the process by which their proudly accumulated mass of possessions (spiritual and material) "shall be scattered abroad in its original atoms" is nearly complete. Their coveted estate is occupied by common people who wrest a living from it with manual labor. One of their scion has married "a young woman of no family or property," lied and left as only heir to the Pyncheon prejudices and delusions a daughter of democracy.

There are but two developments left before the final absorption of the family can be achieved; the working out of each of these is the schedule for the story. By marrying Holgrave, Phoebe must merge, under the healthy and joyous auspices of equalitarianism, the blood of the old Colonel with the blood of the commoner whom he wronged. Thus she will expiate the old social guilt by dissipating the false distinctions that underlay it. Simultaneously the grim pride of the Pyncheons, which has erected as its monument the House of the Seven Gables and maintained the house as a token of inviolateness and aloofness for generations, must be punctured and all its vital juices drawn off until there remains only a monstrous emptiness.

The undemocratic pride of the Pyncheons first manifested itself as sin against society when the Colonel usurped the land of Matthew Maule, the commoner, on which to build a mansion to house his ill-founded pretensions. A self-destructive element in his behavior is implicit in the legend, which attributes his death to the fact that by his conduct he drew on his own head the curse of old Maule. Allegorically considered, Maule's curse is the moral sentence of society which a man inevitably brings on himself in sinning against his fellow. If we read from the legend, then, the sin of pride may be seen to contain the germ of its own annihilation. And if we translate from the legend to the fact in terms of the action of the romance, we shall further see that it is the factor of isolation in the pride of the Pyncheons which automatically effects their ruin.

—Lawrence Sargent Hall, *Hawthorne: Critic of Society* (New Haven: Yale University Press, 1944): pp. 160, 162–163.

[A professor of English at the University of Oregon, Clark
Griffith has also taught at the American University in Cairo,
Egypt. He is the author of *Achilles and the Tortoise: Mark
Twain's Fictions,* and has contributed essays on Poe, Whitman, Dickinson, and other authors to critical journals. In this
essay he discusses how Hawthorne's use of interior and exterior imagery extends throughout the novel.]

Shadow, the past, the inner house—all combine to symbolize the
tragedy of human sin, while the substantial, contemporous world
without provides a warmly optimistic atmosphere in which it seems
possible to conceal this tragedy or to banish it or to live unaware that
it even exists. Such, in turn, are the outlooks, the specious outlooks,
imputed to Jaffrey, Holgrave, and Phoebe.

At first glance, to be sure, any conceptual frame flexible enough to
include these characters, particularly Phoebe and Jaffrey, will seem
highly improbable. Nevertheless, all belong to the world outside the
house and are presented in terms of its key images. Each, for different reasons, resists the profounder implications of the inner house.
As he deals with their respective states of "innocence," Hawthorne's
language, turned now to symbolizing moral positions, remains re-
markably self-consistent. Likening Jaffrey's entire life to a "tall and
stately edifice," he writes that the Judge's sin lurks deep inside, a
"corpse, half decayed, and still decaying . . . with the cobwebs fes-
tooned over its forgotten door." But citizen that he is of the outer
world, Jaffrey never looks inward. To him, as he bluntly reminds
Hepzibah, the past is sheerest nonsense. Around his own impurity
he has arrayed the most imposing of exteriors—a sunny, benevolent
smile and the "splendid halls" and "high cornices" betokening a
guiltless life.

Now despite the signal differences between her and the Judge, it is
noteworthy that Phoebe, too, is regularly associated with images of
sunlight and substantiality; and when closely examined, they turn out
to be not simply the marks of her warm, generous affections. They
symbolize as well the fact that her early responses to the seven-gabled

house curiously parallel Jaffrey's attitude toward his life. Possessing none save the values of the outer world, Phoebe is honestly unprepared to recognize the presence of a "decaying corpse" within. Significantly, she knows little concerning the family's past, has forgotten most of what she once was told, remains profoundly incurious about Clifford's identity, Jaffrey's motives, the meaning of Maule's curse. What Phoebe's "real substance" lacks, as Hawthorne sometimes tries to show, is the modifying influence of tragic insight. While she fails as a character—fails because Hawthorne is only partially capable of demonstrating her maturation—Phoebe is, like Donatello or the bridal pair at Merrymount, an innocent whose defect is her very innocence.

To a considerable extent, therefore, Jaffrey the hypocrite and the guileless Phoebe are less representatives of any particular time than they are traditional character types in Hawthorne's writing; their relation to the outer house is a part of the general symbolic plan. Holgrave, on the other hand, does personify the distinctly modern world beyond the house and, it seems likely, the easy, fallacious ethical perfectionism of the nineteenth century. Like this world of outward forms, he is a thoroughly externalized individual, a figure of many surfaces, forever "putting off one exterior and snatching up another to be soon shifted for a third."

—Clark Griffith, "Substance and Shadow: Language and Meaning in The House of the Seven Gables," *Modern Philology* 51 (February 1954): 189–190.

⊗

MAURICE BEEBE ON SYMBOLISM OF THE HOUSE AND ITS OCCUPANTS

[Author of *Ivory Towers and Sacred Founts: The Artist as Hero in Fiction from Goethe to Joyce,* Maurice Beebe has edited volumes on Ernest Hemingway, William Faulkner, and literary symbolism. He has been a professor of English for many years at Temple University, as well as the editor of *Modern Fiction Studies.* In "The Fall of the House of Pyncheon," he compares Hawthorne's novel to Edgar Allan Poe's short story, "The Fall of the House of Usher," questioning how the relationship between the two works illustrates trends in American fiction. The excerpt below focuses on the multifaceted symbolism of the ancestral home of the Pyncheons.]

Hawthorne places special emphasis on the correspondence between the house and its occupants. ⟨ . . . ⟩

The number *seven* is important in this correspondence. Seven generations of the family have occupied the house: "half a dozen" generations after the founder. As Leland Schubert remarks, there are seven main characters of the present represented in the novel (Clifford, Hepzibah, Judge Pyncheon, Phoebe, Holgrave, Uncle Venner, and Ned Higgins) and seven characters from the past who influence the present (the original Maule, the builder Maule, the carpenter Maule, Alice Pyncheon, Colonel Pyncheon, the storekeeper Pyncheon, and Gervayse Pyncheon). Further support of the correspondence is found in the allusions to man suggested by the number *seven:* man is a creature with seven senses, seven natures, seven vices, and, according to Shakespeare, seven ages. The "sisterhood" of gables calls to mind the once-human Pleiades. Hawthorne did not develop any of these allusions in detail, but he may well have chosen a seven-gabled house as the setting of his novel because *seven* is traditionally associated with human nature.

The peculiarity of the House of Seven Gables is that, like the House of Usher, it seems detached from the world around it. It is the emblem of the human heart, but until the individual human heart is linked to the "comprehensive sympathy above us," it is, like Hepzibah's heart, a dungeon. Maule's Curse is at the root of that "certain remarkable unity" of the Pyncheon family fate, and the house, a product of both Pyncheons and Maules, must remain isolated until the two strains are merged into one. This explains why the symbols of the novel are organized, as Roy Male has shown, in terms of the split between organic and mechanical, spiritual and physical elements in much the same manner as Poe's symbolic "totality" achieves dramatic tension in the conflict between the forces of contradiction and expansion. Symbols of the physical reality, the Actual (the shop bell and devouring Time as represented by the Judge's watch and Ned Higgins) are placed in opposition to symbols which represent the spiritual or Ideal reality (sunshine, fire, and the All-Time of Uncle Venner). Fusing the material and the spiritual are the symbols of moonlight, mirrors, pictures, and the symbolic function of love. The flowers and the fowls are parallel to the Pyncheon house and reveal the changing aspects of the family fortune. ⟨ . . . ⟩

The autobiographical relevance of the novel has been so firmly established by Hawthorne scholars that if we accept the house-human analogy central to the structure of the romance, we may say that the House of Seven Gables *is* Hawthorne and that *The House of the Seven Gables* is the story of his escape or salvation from the curse of isolation. The overt moral of the novel—"the truth, namely, that the wrong-doing of one generation lives into the successive ones, and, divesting itself of every temporary advantage, becomes a pure and uncontrollable mischief"—may seem fanciful to the modern reader, but there is evidence that Hawthorne took it seriously.

—Maurice Beebe, "The Fall of the House of Pyncheon," *Nineteenth-Century Fiction* 11, no. 1 (June 1956): pp. 6–8, 12.

⟨⅊⟩

RICHARD C. CARPENTER ON THE ENDING OF THE NOVEL

[Richard C. Carpenter, a professor of English at Bowling Green State University, is the author of a critical work on Thomas Hardy, as well as numerous essays on Nathaniel Hawthorne, Joseph Conrad, and Thomas Pynchon and on the myth of the hero. In the essay included here, he questions the common critical opinion that the ending of *The House of the Seven Gables* is contrived and unconnected to the rest of the novel. Instead, Carpenter argues, the ending is the careful culmination of plot and characterization, symbolized by Hawthorne's use of flower imagery.]

Throughout the course of the tale a series of horticultural symbols and images which place in opposition the sterility and decay of the elder Pyncheons and the promise of the young couple indicates that fruitful and optimistic outcome is inevitable. ⟨ . . . ⟩

Holgrave, ever curious, has found, "in a garret, over one of the seven gables," some beans which he wishes to test to discover whether there might be a living germ in such ancient seeds. The result of his experiment is a "splendid row of bean vines clambering, early, to the full height of the poles, and arraying them, from top to bottom, in a spiral profusion of red blossoms." To these come the humming-birds, which Clifford watches with "indescribable interest, and even more than childish delight." It is a "wonderful coincidence," so Hepzibah thinks, that Holgrave should have planted these "scarlet-flowering beans—which the humming-birds sought far and wide, and which had not grown in the Pyncheon garden for forty years—on the very summer of Clifford's return."

As readers, however, we should hardly consider this conjunction of circumstances so coincidental as does Hepzibah, for it is patently part of the symbolic plan. Holgrave, turning from his occupation of manipulating the tenuities of light and shade—his character as radical thinker—has brought to fruition both usefulness and beauty. With Phoebe's help (the rule of law emblemized by the office of cultivator) the weedy garden and blighted flowers have given way to the arts of horticulture. In the truest sense the energy of the weeds and the useless beauty of the decadent flowers have been synthesized in a combination which rises above the apparent potentialities of its elements "esemplastically," as Coleridge might have said, producing a new creation. That the bean flowers have kept their fructive energy locked away in darkness and secrecy for these many years emphasizes the latent power of this synthesis. The unbridled growth of the Maule-like weeds has joined with the inutile beauty of the Pyncheon-like flowers to give the climbing, vigorous bean blossoms which are brilliant in their scarlet and promise a future of usefulness.

Thus when we later encounter the handsome barouche and the house in the country, we should not really be disconcerted. The image of the bean flowers is a plain hint of the kind of resolution to be expected, the joining of the Maule and Pyncheon lines in a context of utility.

> —Richard C. Carpenter, "Hawthorne's Scarlet Bean Flowers," *The University Review* 30, no. 1 (October 1963): pp. 65, 69.

[Michael Davitt Bell is a professor of English, American history, and American literature at Williams College. His most influential work, *The Development of Romance: Sacrifice of Relation,* investigates how American romance is connected to other forces in society. He is also the co-author of *Blacks in America.* In this selection he discusses how progress and repetition interact as countervailing forces in *The House of the Seven Gables.*]

⟨T⟩here are tokens of change in the romance as well as tokens of repetition. For example, Holgrave one day tells Phoebe Pyncheon the story of the carpenter, Matthew Maule, grandson of the original "wizard," who hypnotized and eventually destroyed the beautiful Alice Pyncheon. When he has concluded his narrative, Holgrave, a descendant of this Matthew Maule, notices that he, too, has hypnotized a Pyncheon girl, in this case Phoebe. Holgrave's power over Phoebe, Hawthorne tells us, underlining the obvious correspondence between past and present, was as dangerous "as that which the carpenter of his legend had acquired and exercised over the ill-fated Alice." But in the case of this historical correspondence the emphasis is on change rather than repetition. Unlike his carpenter ancestor Holgrave does not take advantage of his power over a beautiful young Pyncheon. Instead of destroying Phoebe, Holgrave finally marries her. This marriage is clearly intended to be contrasted with the abortive relationship of Alice Pyncheon and Matthew Maule, one hundred years before. In this case, it would appear, progress is possible; the past *can be* escaped.

And yet Hawthorne, as narrator, is generally suspicious of the idea of progress in *The House of Seven Gables.* This suspicion can be seen in the skeptical treatment of Holgrave's hopefulness. "It seemed to Holgrave—as doubtless it has seemed to the hopeful of every century, since the epoch of Adam's grandchildren—that in this age, more than ever before, the moss-grown and rotten Past is to be torn down, and lifeless institutions to be thrust out of the way, and their dead corpses buried, and everything to begin anew." Even the belief in progress, Hawthorne hints, is but a cyclically recurring historical phenomenon.

What Holgrave believes has been believed in "every century, since the epoch of Adam's grandchildren." Yet for all his skepticism Hawthorne does not utterly dismiss hopefulness. He qualifies his criticism of Holgrave to say that the artist's error lay not in believing in progress but only in believing in *immediate* progress. "As to the main point—may we never live to doubt it!—as to the better centuries that are coming, the artist was surely right."

And however much Hawthorne intends, in *The House of Seven Gables*, to exhibit the "character of doom," the plot of the book is actually bent on exhibiting the character of hope. The plot of *The House of Seven Gables* is dominated by conventional devices and figures associated with historical progress. Chief among these is the comic marriage plot involving Phoebe and Holgrave. This marriage represents progress not only in contrast with Matthew's treatment of Alice Pyncheon but also in terms of its overall symbolic function of resolving the feud between the Maules and the Pyncheons. For what is this feud between rising democracy and waning aristocracy but the familiar conventional conflict between "liberty" and "tyranny"? This opposition is thoroughly conventional even down to Hawthorne's handling of the witch trials. Matthew Maule, progenitor of the forces of democracy, is condemned by the society of Colonel Pyncheon, progenitor of the forces of tyranny.

—Michael Davitt Bell, *Hawthorne and the Historical Romance of New England* (Princeton: Princeton University Press, 1971): pp. 216–218.

ⓥ

Michael T. Gilmore on Hepzibah's Discomfort

[Michael T. Gilmore is best known for his historical materialist readings of American literature, including *American Romanticism and the Marketplace* and *Rethinking Class: Literary Studies and Social Formations.* He has also written extensively on Kate Chopin, Henry James, Ralph Waldo Emerson, and Herman Melville. He is a professor of English at Brandeis University. The following excerpted essay compares Hepzibah's discomfort with commerce with the position of the writer who must court public approval for his work. Hawthorne himself felt this pressure keenly, and resented that he had to make his art marketable and popular.]

When that shrewd Yankee Dixey passes by the shop, he loudly predicts that Hepzibah's frown will be her financial undoing. "Make it go!" he exclaims. "Not a bit of it! Why her face—I've seen it . . . her face is enough to frighten Old Nick himself, if he had ever so great a mind to trade with her." Overhearing these words, Hepzibah has a painful vision that seems to underscore the futility of her venture. On one side of the street stands her antiquated shop, over which she presides with an offending scowl, and on the other rises a magnificent bazaar, "with a multitude of perfumed and glossy salesmen, smirking, smiling, bowing, and measuring out the goods!" ⟨ . . . ⟩

As such passages suggest, Hawthorne is using Hepzibah to explore his own ambivalence about courting the public in order to make money. Although she herself is not an artist figure, she resembles her creator both in her history of isolation and her need to earn a living. One thinks immediately of Hawthorne's seclusion for thirteen years after graduating from Bowdoin and his self-designation as "the obscurist man of letters in America." It is no wonder that he gives Hepzibah a Puritan progenitor who was involved in the witchcraft trials like his own ancestor John Hathorne, and who appears in his portrait much as William Hathorne is described in "The Custom-House," clutching a Bible and a sword. As an author who always insisted upon preserving "the inmost Me behind its veil," Hawthorne would not have found it difficult to appreciate Hepzibah's misgivings about encountering "the public gaze." He would have understood her resentment at the familiar tone adopted by her customers, who "evidently considered themselves not merely her equals but her patrons and superiors." Indeed, he draws an implicit parallel between his writing and the commodities she hopes to sell. Her stock consists primarily of items of food like apples, Indian meal, and gingerbread men, and in the preface he speaks of his book as an object to be eaten, calling it a "dish offered to the Public." And he seems almost as hesitant about getting his narrative under way as she does about opening her business. Just as she pauses apprehensively on the threshold of her shop, so "we are loitering faint-heartedly," says Hawthorne, "on the threshold of our story."

Despite his sympathy for her discomfort, Hawthorne is far from identifying with Hepzibah uncritically. A part of him yearned "to open an intercourse with the world" and was not above advising his publisher on how to entrap that "great gull," the general reader. This part finds her more comical than tragic and strongly disapproves of her reluctance to seek her own fortune. Although Hawthorne himself had difficulty supporting his family by his writing, and lobbied actively for government appointments, in print he commends the marketplace for fostering self-reliance and expresses detached amusement at Hepzibah's dreams of being rescued from trade by a sudden bequest. Too much of a democrat to endorse her aristocratic pretensions, he agrees with Holgrave that she will discover satisfaction in contributing her mite "to the united struggle of mankind." Her first sale does in fact bring her an unexpected sense of accomplishment and dispels many of her fears about commerce with the world. But she lacks both the skill and the temperament to prosper as a saleswoman, and at the end of the day she has as little to show for "all her painful traffic" as Hawthorne did after his long apprenticeship as a writer of tales and sketches.

—Michael T. Gilmore, "The Artist and the Marketplace in *The House of the Seven Gables*," *ELH* 48, no. 1 (Spring 1981): pp. 176–177.

BRUCE MICHELSON ON HAWTHORNE'S GHOSTS

[A professor of English at the University of Illinois, Bruce Michelson is the author of *Mark Twain on the Loose: A Comic Writer and the American Self,* and *Wilbur's Poetry: Music in a Scattering Time.* In this excerpt he discusses the presence of ghosts and death in *The House of the Seven Gables.*]

When Clifford exclaims, "We are ghosts! We have no right among living beings—no right anywhere but in this old house, which has a curse on it, and which, therefore, we are doomed to haunt!" his remark suggests something more than that he and Hepzibah are too old to change or that they too much resemble the full-time revenants in the mansion. In their ancient silks, turbans, and pallid, dreary gowns, in Hepzibah's scowl and Clifford's ravaged innocent visage, the two strongly recall the period's commonplace engravings of graveyard spirits, but for Hawthorne the resemblance runs much deeper, down to what for Hawthorne was that true ghostliness in which he and we can believe. The vertiginous death-in-life condition of Clifford and Hepzibah—a limbo of ceaselessly repeated actions, of confining temperament, of the same old yearnings frustrated by the same old possibilities—is much more disturbing. The turn-about from the popular haunted house story, that these particular ghosts are more afraid of the outside world than the other way around, only intensifies the menace—which is throughout Hawthorne's work the only otherworldly menace worth worrying about—not that one may be harmed by a ghost but that one may become, by easy, almost imperceptible stages, a ghost oneself.

Through Hepzibah and Clifford, therefore, the popular tradition of the haunted house is linked to Hawthorne's special conception of the revenant and to the moral issue of self-loss through stasis and preservation. Hepzibah and Clifford are the two real haunters of the house; the other two important ghosts in the novel are a good deal more complex, both in their presentation and their importance, and it is chiefly through them that the book takes on its manifold identity. Jaffrey Pyncheon is that special sort of ghost known as the shape-shifter, a far more dangerous sort of spectre to deal with than consistent, timid, and retiring revenants and one that presents an altogether opposite peril to the soul. The danger here is not loss in singlemindedness, reminiscence, reverie but in the disintegration that comes with too much of the public life, of the business of the street, too much attention, in other words, not to the past but to the ideas of poses and the hour. ⟨ . . . ⟩

As Hawthorne had his prolonged sport, in the "Governor Pyncheon" chapter, with Jaffrey's seated corpse, the emphasis falls not simply on this peculiar new serenity, this end to the Judge's perpetual bustling, but also upon the end of all the role playing. The essential hollowness and invisibility of the dead man are harped upon over and over not as new qualities in Jaffrey but as old ones made clear by death. Jaffrey has always been an emptiness inside; the whole, long mock-elegy has as its theme that this void has now lost all disguise. So Hawthorne forestall explicit revelation that Jaffrey has died, for the game he plays first reveals the dead moral sense of the living man and underscores the fact that as far as Jaffrey's true nature is concerned, the dead Judge is not much different from the live one, that the void at the center of Jaffrey, in the spot where the man's soul should be, is not caused but rather discovered by his end. Hawthorne's holiday in the company of Jaffrey's corpse painstakingly chronicles Jaffrey's utter disappearance from the world, the apotheosis of the perfectly invisible man.

—Bruce Michelson, "Hawthorne's House of Three Stories," *The New England Quarterly* 57, no. 2 (June 1984): pp. 168–169, 172–173.

⊗

PETER BUITENHUIS ON THE CHARACTER OF PHOEBE

[After having taught at Yale, the University of California, Berkeley, and McGill University, Peter Buitenhuis is now a professor of English at Simon Fraser University. He has edited many volumes of criticism, among them *French Writers and American Women: Essays by Henry James* and *Five American Moderns: Mary McCarthy, Stephen Crane, J. D. Salinger, Eugene O'Neill, H. L. Mencken*. In this excerpt, he discusses the many symbolic levels behind the characterization of Phoebe.]

The leavening agent in this heavy tale is Phoebe, who has been the subject of much critical discussion. The biographical source for her is obvious: Hawthorne's wife, Sophia, had been instrumental in rescuing him from his spiritual and physical isolation and opening up for him a commerce with the world. She was of a sunny disposition, incurably optimistic, an admirable housekeeper and flower arranger and, like Phoebe, small in body. Moreover, she had urged him to write a brighter book after he had completed the dark and terrible *The Scarlet Letter*. His pet name for her was Phoebe, the small, darting, singing bird common to New England.

The literary origins of Phoebe are also clear. Her prototype is the fair lady of romance tradition, domesticated and sentimentalized by nineteenth-century melodrama. For Hawthorne she is also a symbol of that democratic renewal and energy of the common people that he saw as the transforming agent of the ancestral, aristocratic, and decaying past. She is no thinker, but an active busy housewife who has the knack, like the good fairy, of transforming her surroundings by her presence and disposition. In the novel, she is associated strongly with nature, "as graceful as a bird," Hawthorne writes, "as pleasant, about the house, as a gleam of sunshine falling on the floor through a shadow of twinkling leaves, or as a ray of firelight that dances on the wall, while evening is drawing nigh."

These qualities transform the atmosphere of the House of the Seven Gables: the grime vanishes, the dry rot is stayed, the shadows and the scent of death are banished. Phoebe is the unfallen Eve who restores to Clifford the possibility of life and even happiness. He gazes on her beauty, listens to the sweet sound of her voice, and takes sustenance from her reality. For her part, she is sometimes oppressed by the heavy atmosphere of the house and by Clifford's temperament, but she is loath to explore the riddle of his spiritual and physical enervation and refuses to reflect on it. She is content to tend him and the house and garden so that he can avoid the harsh thoughts of his past, and live in the pleasures of the present.

Phoebe is too good to be true, and Hawthorne is aware that he is sometimes stretching the credulity of his reader in his way of representing her. To justify this minute and sentimental treatment of the minutiae of household life and domestic attentions, he falls back on biblical story and allegory to justify his method. "It was the Eden of a thunder-smitten Adam," he continues, "who had fled for refuge thither out of the same dreary and perilous wilderness, into which the original Adam was expelled." Only when Phoebe returns to her parents' home for a visit is the Edenic blessing suspended, and sin and death can again enter the House of the Seven Gables in the person of Jaffrey Pyncheon.

—Peter Buitenhuis, *The House of the Seven Gables: Severing Family and Colonial Ties* (Boston: Twayne Publishers, 1991): pp. 95–96.

❧

WILLIAM J. SCHEICK ON HAWTHORNE'S IRONIC USE OF GOTHIC CONVENTION

[William J. Scheick is an extremely prolific critic of American fiction. His works include *Design in Puritan American Litera-*

ture, *The Will and the Word: The Poetry of Edward Taylor,* and volumes on seventeenth century American poetry, Cotton Mather, and contemporary American women writers. In this essay he discusses how Hawthorne works to subvert the conventions of Gothic fiction in his novel.]

The breach between exterior appearance and interior impression mentioned in the Preface is manifest in several ways in *The House of the Seven Gables* as structured narrative. One noteworthy example involves the first chapter. This chapter is laden with the devices of Gothic fiction, and it is altogether likely that a reader in Hawthorne's time would have read the introduction as an ostensible promise that the work to follow would fulfill elicited expectations that this work is a Gothic novel. It is a promise not kept, as the reader's encounter with the second chapter begins to indicate. A rupture occurs.

The first chapter is equivalent to the exterior of the seven-gabled house; it is a "ruinous portal" (Gothic tradition), like the "exterior face" of the Pyncheon house, through which we enter the house of the romance. We try to read or interpret this "exterior face" (by way of expectation) even as the characters in the story try to read and interpret on the basis of the outward appearances of the faces they see. We pass through this face-like portal of the first chapter and find our firm sense of material definition and of secure expectation of what is phenomenally real steadily eroded; we are increasingly exposed to the uncertainties of "perplexing mystery," which generate in the "scientific" (matter-oriented) reader a "bewilderment of mind." Passing through the external portal of the first chapter into the interior of romance, the reader experiences what the characters in the romance experience when they enter the Pyncheon house: an incursion into an interior that raises questions about the reality of the external world.

Yet something curious happens. If the romance does not ostensibly fulfill the expectations it stimulates in its first chapter, it does after all *subtly* (as the Preface warned) make good on its promise of a Gothic novel. Although it fails to continue to use the weighty machinery of the Gothic novel and merges Gothic tradition with the domestic and sentimental tradition of the novel, it does, in Gothic tradition, potentially problematize and even destabilize the average reader's sense of the secure nature of phenomenal existence. And the horror here is not one of conventional ghosts; for as the narrator observes, "Ghost-stories are hardly to be treated seriously, any longer." The pause between *seriously* and *any longer* signals the narrator's attitude of irony; as his first chapter indicates, his prospective audience is still very interested in ghost stories, and so his remark is really a warrant, at one level, for the lacuna that occurs in his narrative between his implied promise to present a Gothic story and his actual production. But perhaps even beyond the narrator's knowledge, he has subtly delivered a ghost story, one much more frightening than the conventional ghost story of Gothic fiction.

After the portal-like first chapter, the romance steadily revises Gothic convention by substituting the fantasy of the materialization of some ghost with a still scarier notion that all material entities are already essentially ghosts. As we have seen, the characters and the narrator are each "a substantial emptiness, a material ghost." This revelation is, in accord with the Preface, one subtle message lurking, ghostlike, behind the ostensible Gothic features of the romance. Because it is latent, hidden, like any apparent self, this revelation is itself there and not there—something seemingly substantial as a message, yet really an emptiness signifying the emptiness or absence of human personal identity.

—William J. Scheick, "The Author's Corpse and the Humean Problem of Personal Identity in Hawthorne's *The House of the Seven Gables*," *Studies in the Novel* 24, no. 2 (Summer 1992): pp. 140–141.

Susan S. Williams on Pictures and Portraits

[A professor of English at Ohio State University, Susan S. Williams has published essays in the *Henry James Review, American Quarterly,* and other journals. She is the author of *Confounding Images: Photography and Portraiture in Antebellum American Fiction.* In this essay Williams discusses how portraits in *The House of the Seven Gables* act not as static images but as active agents extending through time. This activity shows that the contrast between visual and literary arts is not as strict as it has often been imagined.]

Seven Gables has "more literal actuality" than Hawthorne's other works. Given Hawthorne's avowed goal, it is significant that he achieves much of this "actuality" by inscribing pictures, and especially portraits, within his text. One of his central characters, Holgrave, makes portraits in his daguerreotype studio, and Colonel Pyncheon assumes a vivid presence through the portrait that memorializes him. Although at times these portraits belong more to the Gothic tradition of the haunted portrait than to a realist tradition, it is important that Hawthorne increases the "minuteness" of his text through the discourse of pictures.

At the same time, *The House of Seven Gables* gives ample evidence of the power of the word. Holgrave is not only a daguerreotypist but also a magazine writer who almost mesmerizes Phoebe as he tells her a story. And the plot relies not only on the topos of the haunted portrait but also on a search for a written deed to a mysterious tract of land—a deed that lies hidden, in fact, behind a painted portrait. Word and image, then, frequently merge in this work, as a writer becomes a daguerreotypist and a portrait covers a written deed. ⟨ . . . ⟩

In *Seven Gables,* however, Hawthorne's sense of the competition between the two arts derives not from their fundamental differences but rather from their similarities. Again and again in the text, portraits are revealed to be animated images living in time—images that contain a narrative of their own. At times these portraits assume a power or "actuality" that supplants that of the subject they represent—the copy replaces the original—or their surface likeness reveals a story or reality invisible in the original. At still other times they seem to reproduce their own copies, both in mental fabrications and in characters who become their doubles. In doing so they become not fixed likenesses but rather living identities that project their subjects into the future. These identities, no less than the controlling narrative, create the action of the plot.

If portraits thus assume some of the traditional properties of narrative in *Seven Gables,* so too does narrative assume some of the properties of portraits. Hawthorne frequently stops the forward progression of his narrative in the text, and he also appeals to characters—especially Phoebe Pyncheon—who are routinized by their conventional attributes, who appear as stock "bodies" rather than as active agents changing in time. Hawthorne uses such convention to control the narrative power of portraits. But in doing so he creates another threat: a fear that this narrative itself—rather than the portraits within it—will become a static, dead work of art. ⟨ . . . ⟩

Colonel's Pyncheon's revenge, of course, is to refuse to stay mute: his portrait animately "speaks" throughout the novel. Only in Holgrave's interpolated tale does it remain mute. This tale, as it describes the mesmerizing voice that Maule has over Alice Pyncheon, is ostensibly about the power of the word; Phoebe also is almost mesmerized while listening to it. But the most important words in the story—the portrait's secret—become frozen into a tableau of occluded speech. At the center of this literary tale, in other words, is a frozen portrait. Narrative in *Seven Gables* tends toward stasis, while much of the true action of the novel is displaced onto "living" portraits.

The fact that Hawthorne's fiction enables him to create these animated portraits, however, seems implicitly to testify to the superiority of the word over the image: the word can subsume images into itself and then displace its own functions onto them. Furthermore, even as the word can make portraits "speak," it can also make them silent. By the end of the novel the portrait of Colonel Pyncheon is again static and mute, lying face down on the floor; its living copy, Judge Pyncheon, is dead; and the real Clifford—as opposed to his real and imaginary portrait—has returned to live with Hepzibah and the newly married Phoebe and Holgrave in a ghost-free country house.

—Susan S. Williams, "'The Aspiring Purpose of an Ambitious Demagogue': Portraiture and *The House of the Seven Gables*," *Nineteenth-Century Literature* 49, no. 2 (September 1994): 221–224, 231–232.

Plot Summary of
The Marble Faun

Published only four years before Hawthorne's death in 1840, *The Marble Faun* was far more difficult for him to write than were his earlier successes, *The Scarlet Letter* and *The House of the Seven Gables.* Based on his wanderings in Europe after his consulship in England, the novel shows evidence of his antipathy toward contemporary Rome, with its "obscure policies and wars," and most particularly its papal authority. *The Marble Faun* is his longest work, as well as the only novel set in Europe; both facts point to a certain tension in its creation. It is neither entirely romantic nor realistic, neither American nor European, neither ultimately cheerful nor powerfully dark. Yet with all of these limitations, *The Marble Faun* possesses extraordinary strengths. Its ambiguity and psychological insight, as well as its great and troublesome central theme, make this one of Hawthorne's most "modern" novels, one disturbingly pertinent today.

The Marble Faun is most concerned with the question of the "fortunate fall," the innocent man caught up in sin who thereby loses his purity but gains, perhaps, a greater moral strength and understanding. Kenyon suggests this understanding of Original Sin when he asks Hilda whether sin is "like sorrow, merely an element of human education, through which we struggle to a higher and purer state than we could otherwise have attained? Did Adam fall, that we might ultimately rise to a far loftier paradise than his?" Donatello, like Adam, gives up his timeless, magical existence for love, murdering Miriam's evil phantom and thus taking on the burden of mortality. In helping her, he becomes wiser and more human, but his newly formed soul is terribly scarred by his actions and their aftermath. Most significantly, he, unlike Dimmesdale in *The Scarlet Letter,* voluntarily accepts his punishment. Hawthorne refuses to completely resolve the question of the moral value of sin and experience one way or the other, an ambivalence that saves the novel from oversimplification and sermonization. Throughout the novel, which was originally titled *Transformation,* he stresses the theme of change and movement, from sketch to painting, from Rome's Etruscan roots to its contemporary Christianity, from the living model to the everlasting marble. Other themes include emotional isolation, the roles and sources of art, the relation of the past to the present, and the corruption and power of the Catholic church.

The structure of *The Marble Faun,* which is like a pattern of rings extending from a stone thrown into a pool, keeps the novel from being a simple tale of sin and redemption. For just as Adam's fall influenced all of humanity, the sin of the murdered monk spreads to encompass all of Hawthorne's characters. The original sin here is Miriam's, the unknown transgression that caused her to flee to Rome. Haunted by the symbol of that sin, the Model, she calls on Donatello to free her, thus enmeshing him in both an old and a new crime. From Miriam and Donatello, the effects of sin move outward to entangle Hilda, Kenyon, and even the Catholic priest who hears Hilda's confession. Each of the characters must thus encounter his or her own Fall, somehow learn from the loss of innocence, and reach redemption. In this way Hawthorne shows the reader that the moral dilemma of human nature is not bounded by the actual commission of sin, but is inherent in existence itself.

Within the larger structure of the widening circle, of course, lies the falling and rising framework of Donatello's sin. Beginning as the innocent, amoral creature of nature, he becomes ever more caught up in human emotions until he pushes the evil specter off the precipice, at which point the novel turns to his penance and ultimate redemption as a full human being.

The story opens upon Miriam, Donatello, Hilda, and Kenyon as they stand in the sculpture gallery of the Capitol in Rome. Looking at a marble statue of a faun carved by the famous Greek sculptor Praxiteles, Miriam exclaims that the sculpture is a perfect portrait of Donatello. The comparison immediately establishes Donatello's connection with the past and Nature, as well as his essential innocence. Hawthorne also introduces his theme of art's relation to life, and the inability of representations to capture the mutability of human nature.

From the gallery, the story flashes back to a visit the four main characters made to the Catacombs of Saint Calixtus. There, amidst the dismal skeletons and decayed altars, Miriam had encountered the mysterious, dark man who haunts them all throughout the novel. She does not explain his connection to her as she leads him out into the light, but his constant presence makes her increasingly melancholy and bad tempered. It is this man who becomes the model for much of Miriam's art, the symbol of sin and evil in the novel.

The introduction of the Model leads immediately to a comparison of Miriam's and Hilda's art. Whereas Miriam's paintings are full of darkness, sexuality, courage, and great originality, Hilda's oils are exquisite, carefully controlled copies of works by the Old Masters. Coming so close after the scene in the catacombs, this comparison suggests that it is Miriam's acquaintance with evil and passion that makes her a superb imaginative artist. Hilda, while very skillful, is only able to channel the power of others.

Leaving Hilda's studio, Miriam walks with Donatello in the meadows and glades surrounding the Villa Borghese. Here they find an impromptu dance in progress, a "Golden Age . . . thawing mankind out of their cold formalities; releasing them from irksome restraint." This is the glorious purity of the past that so enchanted Hawthorne, the idea of sinless people enjoying each other's company without the politics and judgments of real life. However, it is from this joyful state that humans must fall if they are to take part in the world. The Model appears in the dance, leaping like a dark spirit in front of Miriam. Donatello offers to throttle him, but Miriam refuses with a shudder, foreshadowing the later events on the precipice. Miriam goes aside with the Model, who tells her that she will never escape him. "Our fates cross and are entangled. The threads are twisted into a strong cord, which is dragging us to an evil doom." He does not explain further but hints at some stain of blood that clings to her. By leaving their connection, and Miriam's shadowed past, in such ambiguity, Hawthorne both increases suspense and suggests the universality of sin.

Soon after this mysterious interview, Miriam visits Kenyon in his sculpture studio. She gazes at a portrait of Cleopatra he has carved, marveling at his ability to capture the queen's fierce passion, "rapturous enchantment," and tender womanliness. It was his courage and integrity, his willingness to include her burning sexuality, that made the statue great, and it is precisely this courage that he will renounce at the end of the novel. And it is this courage that encourages Miriam to confess her troubles to him. On the verge of speaking, though, she sees the shrinking in his sympathy, his inability to truly help her, and she remains silent.

That night the foursome goes for a moonlit walk through the great ruins of Rome. They pause to look out over the sheer cliff of the Tarpeian Rock, from which traitors were thrown to their deaths in ancient times. When Kenyon goes down the trail, Hilda notices that Miriam has remained behind, and she turns back to rejoin her friend and Donatello. She arrives just in time to see Donatello, enraged by the sudden and ominous appearance of the Model, push the evil figure over the precipice. Horrified, she rushes away, as Miriam stares wildly at Donatello. The significance of the crime is immediate: "It had kindled [Donatello] into a man; it had developed within him an intelligence which was no native characteristic of the Donatello we have heretofore known. But that simple and joyous creature was gone forever."

Miriam herself is deeply affected by the murder, which she feels she caused Donatello to commit. She goes to Hilda to seek forgiveness and support, but Hilda repels her friend's advances. Her coldness is closely linked to her impregnable purity, but nonetheless seems cruel and almost inhuman.

That summer Kenyon goes to visit Donatello in the faun's family home of Monte Beni, in the Tuscan countryside. The young man is deeply depressed, transformed by his murderous rage and subsequent contrition. He is unable to find joy in the magical golden wine of his vineyards, unable to commune with the animals in his forests as he did when a child. Kenyon convinces him to go for a journey to Perugia to break out of his morbid solitude, and the two men travel through the small towns and valleys. They are secretly accompanied by Miriam, who is determined to save Donatello from the fate her presence brought upon him. They meet at the fountain of the market town, where Miriam and Donatello confess their continuing love for each other. Kenyon, however, refuses to allow the possibility of earthly joy in the face of their guilty past. They must be like brother and sister, but bound together by both love and a life of penitence and prayer. To Hawthorne, sin can never be avoided or ignored; it must be atoned for through painful contrition.

Meanwhile Hilda has also been crushed by her loss of innocence. Lonely and frightened, she takes refuge in the church of St. Peter's. She enters the confessional and reveals her secret to a priest, a shocking act for an American Protestant in Hawthorne's day. Instantly relieved, she feels herself as pure as she was in her childhood. She takes up once again her friendship with Kenyon, who has returned from Tuscany, and the two discuss the fate of Miriam and Donatello. Kenyon suggests that good may have resulted from their crime, a view Hilda indignantly denies. Shortly after this, Hilda mysteriously disappears, leaving Kenyon terribly worried.

While out walking in the fields, he meets Miriam and Donatello, who assure him that Hilda is safe, but will not tell him where she is. Two days after this meeting, the three meet once again, this time in the streets of Rome. It is Carnival time, and the gaily costumed crowds provide a surreal backdrop to the final scene of reunion between Kenyon and Hilda. She tells him that she was held prisoner in a convent by government officials who suspected some political intrigue surrounding her relationship with Miriam, who had powerful family connections in Rome. In the end, Kenyon and Hilda return to America contentedly married, Miriam goes abroad to expiate her sin in solitary penance, and Donatello gives himself up to life in prison. ❀

List of Characters in
The Marble Faun

At the beginning of *The Marble Faun,* **Donatello** is the figure of perfect innocence. His resemblance to the marble statue of the title suggests both his mystical nature and his lack of connection to humanity. The young Italian is like a child, unacquainted with evil and virtually unable to make moral distinctions. In his purity, he is both more and less than human. Yet later in the story Hawthorne reveals that Donatello is also the Count of Monte Beni, the sole heir to an ancient family of Tuscan nobles. His family claims an ancestor drawn from Greek myth, a faun like the legendary Pan. This link with nature increases Donatello's purity, but also the capacity for uncontrolled passion shown in the murder of the monk. It is Donatello's transformation from magical, sylvan faun into "a man of feeling and intelligence," via an exposure to evil, that lies at the heart of the romance.

Miriam's enormous complexity and mystery act in contrast to Donatello's characterization. She is a painter who appeared in Rome with no explanation of her origins, causing speculation that she was either the heiress of a Jewish banker, a German princess, or the daughter of an American planter. This ambiguity lends Miriam an air of dark secrecy, quite at odds with Donatello's fanciful origins. Miriam's grim, psychologically complex paintings also act as an antithesis to Hilda's virginal innocence. She is neurotically passionate, but this passion lends her art a symbolic depth and imaginativeness that Hilda shrinks from encountering. Miriam is also one of Hawthorne's strongest female characters, bearing the torment of the model's presence, and the sin of his death, with the fortitude of the indomitable biblical women she is so fond of painting. Her tragic fate, her ability to take on various characterizations and her secret guilt, all work to cast Miriam as a romantic heroine.

Hilda's most important feature is her virginity. She is pure not only sexually but morally, unable to acknowledge the existence of evil in the world. Hilda has come from America to Rome to paint, but finds her imagination thwarted by the influence of the Old Masters who have gone before her. She decides to become a copyist, creating beautiful reproductions of famous paintings. Living in a tower, far from the bustle and commerce of the street, Hilda is attended by a flock of white doves as she tends an eternal flame dedicated to the Virgin Mother. In her constant purity, Hilda is to some extent an allegorical character, symbolizing Purity, the Virgin Mary, or perhaps idealized Femininity. Her uncompromising judgment on Miriam's sin makes her seem almost as inhuman as Donatello, and in the end both characters have become more complex through their exposure to sin. Hilda is also the representative of American Protestantism within Catholic Rome. While she goes to the church to seek spiritual peace, she rejects the overtures of the priest who seeks to convert her.

A young American sculptor, **Kenyon** occupies a place midway between Miriam and Hilda. He is more worldly than Hilda, more able to see the good resulting from Donatello's and Miriam's sins, but his prudishness aligns him more with the young American painter than the fated couple. He sermonizes at the two after their reunion, denying them any possibility of joy or the support of marriage, yet his consistent concern for Donatello makes him nonetheless a sympathetic character. Kenyon is the most observant of the characters, able to step back and analyze the situation to make sense of it. His intellect, combined with his spiritual love of Hilda, help the reader both understand and feel sympathy for the action of the romance. However, in the end Kenyon is the least affected by the events of the tale, the least transformed. His only true change is his repudiation of his art, an action seriously suspect in Hawthorne's universe.

The Model is a dark man who haunts Miriam's footsteps; he is almost a caricature of evil. This obscure figure from Miriam's earlier life, cloaked and bearded like a classic portrait of the devil, appears in the catacombs symbolically surrounded by death. From then on he haunts Miriam, who refuses to explain who he is. She paints him over and over, unable to banish him from her art. Hawthorne reveals late in the novel that he is her former fiancé, a treacherous madman whom she fled to Rome to escape. The spectre himself says that he has a power over Miriam, though the reader is never told what that power is. Soon it seems that she has become virtually his slave. As the character of Evil, the Model suggests to Miriam that the only way she will be able to free herself from him is by murdering him, thus giving her the option of lifelong torment or terrible sin. The Model never takes on any human qualities, and thus cannot achieve the level of realism and interest of the other characters. After his death, Miriam finds that the Model had become a Capuchin monk, Father Antonio, who was noted for his "unusual sanctity." The contrast between this holy profession and the wickedness he causes lends a final level of irony to his characterization. ❀

Critical Views of
The Marble Faun

R. W. B. Lewis on Donatello as Hero of the Hopeful

[A professor of English and American Studies at Yale University, R. W. B. Lewis was also the literature consultant to Universal Pictures. His most renowned work, *Edith Wharton: A Biography,* earned Lewis the Pulitzer, Bancroft, and National Book Critics Circle awards for 1976. He is also the author of *The Picaresque Saint: Representative Figures in Contemporary Fiction* and volumes on Melville, Whitman, and Malraux. In this excerpt he compares Donatello to other classically innocent American heroes such as Billy Budd, and explores the impact of time on this innocence.]

Donatello in *The Marble Faun* is the most innocent person and the figure least conscious of the force and challenge of time in nineteenth-century American literature, with the exception of Billy Budd. And he is introduced in the midst of an immeasurable and continuously influential antiquity—an antiquity which touches him not at all, until he has sinned. 〈 . . . 〉

That action is the transformation of the soul in its journey from innocence to conscience: the soul's realization of itself under the impact of and by engagement with evil—the tragic rise born of the fortunate fall. It is a New World action—my supposition is that it is *the* New World action, the tragic remainder of what Lawrence called the myth of America. It is what has to happen to "golden youth" if it is to mature; and the novel is the kind of novel which had to be written if the young literature was to mature. Donatello, though purportedly an Italian aristocrat, is nonetheless the hero of the hopeful, seen in a tragic perspective: the figure who, in approaching experience, comes up against the social world under the great, appealing illusion that (in the words of Horace Bushnell) he is "a free person [who has] just begun to be." 〈 . . . 〉

The action has to do with the discovery of *time* as a metaphor of the experience of evil. Rome is thus the best imaginable setting; nothing in the New World could match it. What was wanted, for the maximum effect, was maximum antiquity—a symbol coexistent, if possible, with the temporal order itself; and Rome is identified in the story as "the city of all time." The seven-gabled home of the Pyncheons had reached back a century or so to the Puritan period, and Hawthorne did all he could with it. But Rome, Hawthorne remarks on the opening page of *The Marble Faun*, reaches back through a "threefold antiquity"— Christian, Roman, Etruscan. And it is in dramatic contrast to such massive age that the hero is then promptly introduced as an "Arcadian simpleton." ⟨ . . . ⟩ It is thus only *after* the sin and the flight that Donatello seems to grow aware of his own ancestry—explaining to Kenyon, at Monte Beni, that his family history goes back beyond the Middle Ages to earliest Christendom and perhaps to a time before that. Donatello's family, like the city of Rome, has a multiple antiquity; and his acceptance of the burden of inheritance may be his way of coming to terms with all that Rome represents in the novel: with the world.

The degree of actual tension in *The Marble Faun* is the degree of Hawthorne's divided sympathies toward the contending factors. And he was not less ambivalent toward time then he had been toward the Puritan community. His involvement with time, always profound, had always been notably ambiguous. It was not a metaphysical interest; Hawthorne had been concerned not with the ontological status of time, but with its contents and effects: not with time as a concept, but with the coloration it lent to the things it perpetuated and with the value or the misfortune of sustained temporal relations. He had a passion for sources and beginnings, for traditions and continuities, and resented in America the scantiness of histories. Though Tocqueville was unduly impressed by the claims of the hopeful and had doubted that American poetry would "be fed with legends or the memorials of old tradition," Hawthorne never seemed able to get hold of legends and traditions enough. He wore out the few he could find; and it may have been to refurbish his stock that in 1853 he consented to go to Europe as his government's representative. In Europe, where he tripped over unchanging traditions and customs in appalling abundance, his resentment veered around toward the ancient.

—R. W. B. Lewis, *The American Adam: Innocence, Tragedy and Tradition in the Nineteenth Century* (Chicago: University of Chicago Press, 1955): pp. 121–123.

Peter G. Beidler on the Change in Donatello

[Peter Beidler, the Distinguished Professor of English at Lehigh University, has taught American literature and Native American studies. He is the author of *Ghosts, Demons and Henry James, Fig Tree John: An American Indian in Fact and Fiction,* and *Masculinities in Chaucer.* In this excerpt he questions whether the change in Donatello from innocence to knowledge is in fact a "fortunate" fall.]

There are, I believe, four distinct questions involved in the theme of the fortunate fall, and the only way that we can get at what Hawthorne is about in the novel is to discuss each one separately. The first question concerns the development of Donatello. Does he rise as a result of his sin and the suffering that sin caused? In other words, does sin educate him? I think that Hawthorne's answer to this one is a clear affirmative: Donatello does gain in moral and intellectual perception as a result of his sin. The author, Miriam, Kenyon, and Hilda all express at least once their awareness of Donatello's growth. The author, speaking clearly in an authorial voice, notes that the "fierce energy" which inspired Donatello immediately after his crime "had kindled him into a man; it had developed within him an intelligence which was no native characteristic of the Donatello whom we have heretofore known." A little later he tells us that "in the black depths, the Faun had found a soul, and was struggling with it towards the light of heaven." 〈 . . . 〉

The second question is closely related to the first. If sin educated Donatello, is sin then the *only* means of education? This, we remember, is Miriam's first question to Kenyon: did Donatello's sin bring his "simple and imperfect nature to a point of feeling and intelligence which it could have reached under no other discipline?" Kenyon refuses to agree with her. Nor should we have expected him to, for he had earlier mused that "sometimes, perhaps, the instruction comes without the sorrow." While Kenyon does not question that sin *has* educated Donatello, he is not willing to say that therefore sin *alone* could have educated him. A man might be educated in other ways also. I see no reason to think that Hawthorne did not agree with Kenyon here. Miriam is the only one who explicitly holds the opposite view, and she, as we shall see later, is given to some rather questionable speculation here at the end of the novel.

The third question is not answered so positively. Was Donatello's education, his growth, good as it unquestionably was, worth the sacrifice of the old Donatello? . . . The author, for example, suggests that a little of Donatello's simplicity might profitably be fused into other men, "might partly restore what man has lost of the divine." And immediately after telling us that Donatello developed "an intelligence which was no native characteristic of the Donatello we have heretofore known" he adds "but that simple and joyous creature was gone forever." . . . Kenyon, however, is the chief spokesman for the view that Donatello's education might not have been worth the sacrifice. Human beings, he says, "are getting so far beyond the childhood of their race that they scorn to be happy any longer." . . . It seems clear that Hawthorne does not want us to ignore the sacrifice that Donatello was forced to make for his growth. . . . Donatello's growth was both good and bad, or, to put in Hawthorne's words, those who descend into the caverns emerge from them with both "truer and sadder views of life forever afterwards." To insist that such views are *only* truer or *only* sadder is to do an injustice to the novel.

We come, then, to the fourth question: Was Adam's fall part of a divine plan by which we might all rise to greater moral and intellectual heights? We cannot help noticing that Miriam is the only one to hold this view. ⟨S⟩ince the author avoids any direct comment, we might feel free to question the logicality of Miriam's view. What, after all, is it based on? Inductive reasoning is reasoning from specific cases to a general principle. But Miriam has only one case to reason from, Donatello's. Her reasoning, then, would run something like this: Donatello's sin brought about certain worthwhile changes in him; therefore sin brings about worthwhile changes in all men, and since Adam was the archetypal man, Adam's sin was fortunate. Her inductive leap lands her on a pretty precarious cliff. Her reasoning is rendered even more shaky when we note that she has apparently ignored the fact that Donatello's sin also brought about changes in him which were not fortunate.

—Peter G. Beidler, "Theme of the Fortunate Fall in *The Marble Faun*," *Emerson Society Quarterly* 47, no. 2 (second quarter 1967): 59–61.

[One of the most prolific of modern American critics, Sacvan Bercovitch is a professor of English at Harvard University. He is the general editor of the *Cambridge History of American Literature,* and the author of *Typology and Early American Literature, Puritan Origins of the American Self, Reconstructing American Literary History,* and other works. Here he explains why Hilda refuses to help Miriam, an action that seems strangely cruel and cold to many readers.]

Perhaps the dominant image of Hilda pictures her as the custodian of the Virgin's Shrine. Every aspect of her description supports the image: her white robe, the tower she lives in and the doves she feeds, her vocation as copyist—and, most directly, her devoted tending of the eternal flame. She "religiously lit" and "trimmed the lamp before the Virgin's shrine," writes Hawthorne over and again, and kept "the flame of the never-dying lamp . . . burning at noon, at *midnight,* and at all hours of the twenty-four" (my italics). Professor Fogle finds in these passages an evocation of the vestal virgins, transformed in terms of Christian worship. More specifically, they seem to refer to the faithful virgins in Matthew, who prepared their lamps with care, so that when the "bridegroom" appeared "at midnight" they could rise ready to "go . . . out to meet him." Like them, Hilda guards her virtue "in an evil world"; like them, she resolves to wear her white robe "back to Him"; and like them, she turns away the sinner who seeks her aid. The parable, we recall, tells of ten virgins

> which took their lamps, and went forth to meet the bridegroom. And five of them were wise, and five *were* foolish. They that *were* foolish . . . took no oil with them: But the wise took oil in their vessels with the lamps. While the bridegroom tarried, they all . . . slept. And at midnight there was a cry made, Behold, the bridegroom cometh. . . . Then all those virgins arose. . . . And the foolish said to the wise, Give us of your oil; for our lamps are gone out. But the wise answered, saying, *Not so:* lest there be not enough for us and you; but go ye rather to them that sell, and buy for yourselves. (Matt. 5:1-9)

From this perspective, Hilda's action becomes at least morally intelligible. She recognizes her frailty and dares not jeopardize the little grace granted to "a poor, lonely girl." A wise virgin, she decides to leave the dispensation to God. She refuses Miriam not out of hardheartedness but in the conviction that she is impotent to "save" her, that her foolish friend must find her own way "to them that sell, and buy" for herself. ⟨ . . . ⟩

In short, the denial stems both from humility and from true Christian compassion: the wise virgins "consider that God has now broken open the consciences of the foolish"; they understand, furthermore, that "other means are sanctified to beget Grace . . . or rather a greater efficacy and power; hence they send them to other means."

It would be too much to say that Hilda—"daughter of the Puritans" though she is—reasons all this through when she sends Miriam from her studio. Yet surely she senses it on some half-conscious level. Though she never presumes to forgive, she prays that Miriam will receive pity and grace through "a greater efficacy and power"; though she reproves Kenyon for his *felix culpa* conjectures, her heart goes out (immediately afterwards) to the "kneeling figure" of Miriam—now a "female penitent" with "upturned face"—extending "her hands with a gesture of benediction"; and though the author cannot tell us at the end "what . . . Miriam's life [was] to be," he assures us that "Hilda had a hopeful soul, and saw sunlight on the mountaintops." This optimism does not altogether justify Hilda. She, too, requires "a sin to soften" her, and, in token of her softening, must come "down from her old tower," leaving it to "another hand . . . henceforth [to] trim the lamp before the Virgin's shrine." But her hopefulness does serve, retrospectively, a positive function. For all Hawthorne's reticence in the matter, it throws doubt on Miriam's despair before the closed window; and despite his insistence on Hilda's "simplicity," it casts a gentler light on her judgment when, with instinctive benevolence, she helped direct a distraught friend to face her guilt, to seek mercy "from Him that hath the Spirit without measure," and thereby, perhaps to find her dark and lonely way to redemption.

—Sacvan Bercovitch, "Of Wise and Foolish Virgins: Hilda versus Miriam in Hawthorne's *Marble Faun*," *The New England Quarterly* XLI, no. 2 (June 1968): pp. 282–283, 285–286.

[Joel Porte is a professor of English and American literature at Cornell University. He is the author of *Emerson and Thoreau: Transcendentalists in Conflict* and *Representative Man: Ralph Waldo Emerson in His Time*. He has also written numerous articles on Emerson, Thoreau, Gothic fiction, and Henry James. Here he explores how Hilda's inability to face evil and experience limits her as an artist.]

Hawthorne's constant preoccupation with the function of the artist, so intimately connected with the whole notion of romance, engrossed him to such a degree by the time of *The Marble Faun* that it at last became the actual subject of his book. All four of the protagonists are, literally or metaphorically, artists; and the tale is essentially devoted to describing the relationship between individual experience and its reflection in art, which is seen as both the key to and an expression of character. The romancer's belief in the living force of true art—that is, art based on profound human experience—is embodied by Hawthorne in the very person of his eponymous hero. Donatello, who bears a sculptor's name, is shown in the course of the action to be the creator of his new self. He transforms himself (and *Transformation* was the title given the book by Hawthorne's English publishers) from a statue, the innocent marble faun, into a sinful adult man by a conscious act of will—demonstrating, as it were, that all that is needed to make art truly alive is the touch of suffering humanity.

Just as Donatello becomes the human emblem of a truth about art, so artistic objects are used to emblematize the human meaning of his transformation. Walking through the Capitoline Museum in the opening scene of the book, Miriam, Hilda, and Kenyon are struck by Donatello's resemblance to the Faun of the Praxiteles. But while they are discussing this fancied similarity, Donatello shows a decided propensity for circling around the statue of the Dying Gladiator (the first object described by Hawthorne when the four friends entered the museum). Thus, briefly but tellingly, Hawthorne suggests Donatello's fate as a living piece of sculpture—from a young and simple prelapsarian faun to a tragic warrior who discovers his own mortality in the act of bringing death to another. The inverse case of Hilda (an example of obstinate non-transformation) is also prefigured in Hawthorne's presentation of a statue showing "the Human Soul, with its choice of Innocence or Evil close at hand, in the pretty figure of a child, clasping a dove to her bosom, but assaulted by a snake." No other sculpture is described to foretell a change in Hilda's symbolic posture; and she does indeed begin and end as a child, desperately clutching her dove in the face of omnipresent evil. ⟨ . . . ⟩

The most significant thing about Hilda's artistry is that, in sharp distinction to Miriam's powerful and terrible originality, she is a copyist. ⟨ . . . ⟩

Original art, as in Miriam's case, demands an exposure of the secret self that Hilda is not prepared to make. And it is also predicated on an openness to experience, a willingness to gaze steadily at all possibilities of existence, that is alien to Hilda's virginal nature. Examining a cartoon which presumably represents Guido's "original sketch for the picture of the Archangel Michael, setting his foot upon the demon," Hilda reverently describes "the Archangel, who turns away his eyes in painful disgust" from the vindictive scowl of the demon, whereupon Miriam laughs to scorn the "daintiness" of Guido's Michael: "He never could have looked that Demon in the face!" Hilda is predictably shocked at Miriam's irreverence, but the full measure of Hilda's devotion to Guido's Archangel—in her opinion, "the most beautiful and the divinest figure that mortal painter ever drew"—becomes clear only later in the book, when she prays to him in her trouble. For Guido's Michael, in his desire to oppose evil but not to gaze on it, is the perfect emblem of Hilda's own nature.

—Joel Porte, *The Romance in America: Studies in Cooper, Poe, Hawthorne, Melville and James* (Middletown, Conn: Wesleyan University Press, 1969): pp. 138–139, 142–143.

⟨ⱴ⟩

NINA BAYM ON KENYON'S STORY

[Nina Baym is one of the best-known feminist scholars in America, as well as a noted critic of American literature. She has received fellowships from the Guggenheim Foundation and the National Endowment for the Humanities, and has been an associate of the Center for Advanced Studies at Princeton University. Since 1963 she has been a Liberal Arts and Sciences Jubilee Professor of English at the University of Illinois at Urbana-Champaign. She is the author of *The Shape of Hawthorne's Career, Women's Fiction: A Guide to Novels By and About Women, 1820–1870,* and *Feminism and American Literary History: Essays.* She is the co-editor of the *Norton Anthology of American Literature* and the *Columbia History of the United States.* In this essay she explains how Kenyon acts as the center of *The Marble Faun,* symbolizing the pressures of the Eros and control on the artist.]

As in the other three romances, the plot coheres around a character who stands a little apart from the action. Though he appears almost a bystander, the narrative is ultimately his because all events in it derive their true significance from their effect on and meaning for him. Kenyon's story is—like Dimmesdale's, Holgrave's, and Coverdale's—the story of the failed or destroyed artist. A young American sculptor of considerable promise, he goes to Rome to develop his talent. He is, however, ignorant and innocent; he does not really know either what art is or what demands it makes on the artist. In Rome he becomes involved in the lives of two mysterious and beautiful Europeans—Miriam and Donatello—whose symbolic function is to teach him those things he does not know and to offer him the gift of great artistic powers if he masters their teachings. The artist's creative powers, he learns, are one with the life force that permeates nature. They rise from the subterranean depths of the self, are essentially erotic in character, and thoroughly abhorrent to society. The lesson terrifies him, and he flees backwards towards the safety represented by Hilda. Her virginal conventionality is antithetical to the disruptive sensuality of Miriam and Donatello; in his shattered, enervated panic, Kenyon gladly makes the exchange. ⟨ . . . ⟩

⟨Much⟩ is at stake in the question of Kenyon's development as an artist. His Cleopatra, produced in the seething excitement of exposure to masterpieces, solves certain problems peculiar to the sculptor's medium (catching life in stone, transmitting action in a reposing figure) but is especially noteworthy for its effective handling of costume and even more for its undistinguished celebration of Cleopatra's anarchically erotic nature. When he begins working on the bust of Donatello, Kenyon makes yet another advance, going beyond Cleopatra's simple eroticism into something far more complex and timely. For he now perceives beauty and virtue in the very qualities of Donatello that are "fallen." The uncomplicated classical or preclassical beauty of the faun strikes him as vapid and monotonous; Donatello has become beautified and moralized precisely through his act of rebellion, an act totally outside the experience of pagan man, and therefore not represented in the features of pagan statues. Since Kenyon believes that sin cannot coexist with beauty, he is led intuitively to believe that Donatello and his Monte Beni are, though fallen, sinless. The fall of man is the story of man's growth from innocent prettiness to moral beauty, rather than from innocent beauty to sinful ugliness. This is an intuition which can make Kenyon a very great artist; it is also social heresy, but Kenyon does not begin at this point to sense its dangerous social implications. ⟨ . . . ⟩

⟨T⟩he conclusion of the book, when Kenyon once again raises his heretical ideas, this time formally to repudiate them as the price of Hilda's hand. Or it may be the surfacing of insupportable sexual anxiety, as suggested in the grotesque figures that attack him during the carnival. Whatever the cause, it is clear that Miriam and Donatello are not worth the emotional cost to Kenyon that is represented by his loss of Hilda. ⟨ . . . ⟩

⟨Miriam and Donatello⟩ are the power within him that can grasp and create great art. But Kenyon is no longer able to use the faculty they personify. Once briefly united with them, he is now irrevocably sundered from them. He explains his sudden change, his revulsion from art and his choice of Hilda, by identifying Hilda with life and the Venus with dead marble. Frederick Crews put it admirably: Hawthorne "seems to be saying that Kenyon's human love is supplanting his cold aesthetic taste. . . . Yet when we reflect that vapid Hilda is here dethroning a supple and lovely Venus, the surfacing meaning becomes exactly reversed." The "surface meaning" is no more than Kenyon's neurotic rationalization; victim of his age's malaise, he chooses the Virgin over Venus, a commitment which as Crews says is "simply a form of panic."

—Nina Baym, "*The Marble Faun:* Hawthorne's Elegy for Art," *The New England Quarterly* XLIV, no. 3 (September 1971): pp. 355–356, 363–364, 372–374.

James G. Janssen on the Transformation of Donatello

[James G. Janssen is a professor of American literature at Arizona State University and a member of the Hawthorne Society of America. His articles on Hawthorne have appeared in the *Nathaniel Hawthorne Journal, Studies in American Humor,* and the *Emerson Society Quarterly.* In this essay he discusses how wisdom and joy combine in the transformation of Donatello from faun to human.]

If earlier in the book Donatello had lived only in the present, and was incapable of thinking of the future, he now has an awareness of the past, present, and future that is a frame of reference against which man's potential for good and evil can be seen and measured—an awareness combining the tragic and the comic. Miriam had once warned Donatello that, if he stayed too long in Rome, he would become as wide and as wretched as all mankind. That transformation or education into an enlarged sensibility, begun as soon as he commits his crime on behalf of Miriam, reaches its most obvious state when, at the end of the book, Donatello's attitudes are characterized by a "playfulness [that] came out of his heart, and glimmered like firelight on his actions, alternating, or even closely intermingled, with profound sympathy and serious thought." ⟨ . . . ⟩

It is interesting that Miriam, in observing this change in Donatello's manner, is prompted to introduce for the first time the formal idea that his transformation has come about by means of a happy fault, in that out of his guilt has come a greater sensitivity—in terms of this study, a nature that has gone from mere sportiveness to a thoughtful acknowledgment of the light *and* the dark. It may not be too much to suggest that the very nature of the *felix culpa* concept is, if not a "humorous" notion, at least one that has a whimsical, fanciful character, one that we can expect took a certain amount of "playfulness" in its first paradoxical expression ⟨. . . . ⟩

Such a mood of incongruity is clearly prevalent in the final act of *The Marble Faun,* set as it is against the richly ambiguous images of the Roman carnival. The featured player is Kenyon, who finds himself at first at odds with the festive atmosphere, but who is eventually reunited with Hilda and sees the drama come to a close in the imprisonment of Donatello, the banishment of Miriam to her own psychological dungeon, and the promise of marriage for himself and Hilda.

As in an earlier passage in which Miriam and Donatello are associated with a "deeper joy," Hawthorne begins this segment of the book with a vaguely philosophical comment on the profounder truth that allows an element of the merry to highlight the more somber threads of life. In an apparent reference to Kenyon, who in his distress over the disappearance of Hilda is very much at odds with the carnival spirit— as, apparently, are all men whose dark cast of mind allows them to see only sable images—Hawthorne makes a number of interesting if difficult distinctions. First of all, he seems to suggest that the present carnival is only a pale continuation of the former robust jollity that inspired it: "if decrepit and melancholy Rome smiles, and laughs broadly, indeed, at Carnival-time, it is not in the old simplicity of real mirth, but with a half-conscious effort, like our self-deceptive pretense of jollity at a threadbare joke." If this passage is read superficially, Hawthorne seems here to be criticizing "invented" moods of joy that lack genuine feeling; he seems, too, to be approving of Donatello's previous "simple" state of unreflective sportiveness, against the argument that has been advanced in these pages that the kind of fused mood characteristic of Miriam is somehow more valuable and mature.

But just as we begin to doubt our original interpretation, Hawthorne provides a key idea that confirms it: that whatever its present character, mankind had better avail itself of those opportunities left to enjoy. For "there is a Wisdom that looks grave, and sneers at merriment; and again a *deeper Wisdom,* that stoops to be gay as often as occasion serves, and oftenest avails itself of shallow and trifling grounds of mirth; because, if we wait for more substantial ones, we seldom can be gay at all. Therefore, had it been possible, Kenyon would have done well to mask himself in some wild, hairy visage, and plunge into the throng of other masquers, as at the Carnival before" (italics mine). It will be noted, first of all, that what was previously termed "deeper joy" has now become "deeper Wisdom," more directly indicating not just a state of emotional well-being but an intellectual gain. It does not seem plausible that in either term Hawthorne is suggesting anything as superficial as mere escapism from tragedy into an uncaring, unreflective, blind frolic; nor is the mood exactly that of *carpe diem;* nor is it mere "comic relief." The phrase seems rather to indicate a philosophical outlook Hawthorne considers most promising, even necessary—an outlook which takes ample note of the discrepancy between human expectation on the one hand, and man's limited potential for fulfillment on the other, the recognition of which is for man one of his most characteristically dismal—and noble—moments of awareness. Not entirely like or unlike the more contemporary mood in literature called "dark humor," it is inspired by a view neither nihilistic nor pessimistic, but by an inevitable assessment of a human race that has fallen—but not very far—from grace; and which, paradoxically, has gained in the process!

—James G. Janssen, "The 'Grim Identity' in Hawthorne's *Marble Faun*," *Studies in the Novel* 15, no. 2 (Summer 1983): pp. 116–119.

⊛

DARRELL ABEL CONTRASTS THE SPECTRE WITH THE FAUN

[A professor of English at Purdue University and Franklin and Marshall College, Darrell Abel is a well-known critic of early American literature. His publications include *Colonial and Early National Writing* and *Masterworks of American Realism*. In this section of *The Moral Picturesque* he shows how the Model in *The Marble Faun* symbolizes the negative pressures of time and history.]

Just as the Faun is a symbol of man's instinctive presence in nature, so is the Spectre of the Catacomb (Miriam's model) a symbol of man's beguilment into a world of abstractive thought. Instead of joyous participation in the instant life of nature, his existence is a gloomy isolation in an introspective egoism, his consciousness peopled by phantoms from a remembered past. The Faun and the Spectre are at opposite extremes in the range of sophistication. In Hawthorne's figure of the human heart "allegorized as a cavern; at the entrance . . . sunshine and flowers . . . Within, . . . a terrible gloom and monsters," which occurs in an early entry in his notebooks, these expressionistic characters are figured. The Faun is human nature among the sunshine and flowers at the entrance to this unexplored cavern of the heart; the Spectre is a monster that haunts the terrible gloom within. The Faun expresses man's delight in a vivid present that insistently solicits the senses; the Spectre man's sorrow over a shadowy past that irrepressibly haunts the mind. The world as it exists to the apprehension of the Spectre is a Tomb. He is one "to whom midnight would be more congenial that noonday." He is associated with darkness, as the Faun is with sunshine.

The Spectre distinguishes his reality through the faculty of memory; the past determines the character of the present and future for him, so that his characteristic activity is following someone. His relentless pursuit of Miriam typifies what Hawthorne described in "Monsieur du Miroir" as the "hopeless race that men sometimes run with memory, or their own hearts, or their moral selves." Memory perpetuates every evil and error enacted in life, and extends their operation through time to come. Ugliness that in the natural course of events would be purged from the system of things is carried along by memory as the determining principle in emergent actuality. The Spectre would "gratify his fiendish malignity . . . by perhaps bringing some old pestilence or other forgotten and long-buried evil on society; or possibly, teaching the modern world some decayed and dusty kind of crime which the antique Romans knew; and then would hasten back to the catacomb."

The concepts of memory and time combine to give an individual self-consciousness and age—for age is the appreciable duration in time of an individual thing. The Faun, as we have remarked, was ageless because he lacked the conception of his distinct identity through a past, a present, and a future. The Spectre, in contrast, was aged. The Faun's life was a perpetual renovation of humanity, but the Spectre's exemplifies the persistence of the ego. Instead of submitting himself to being converted "back to the sympathies from which human existence had estranged" him, and rising again to sentience as a fresh manifestation of vital reality, he has resisted death and thereby paradoxically resisted life and prolonged his mortality. He pursued other human beings in order to "beguile new victims into his own misery"—that is, to withdraw them from life (which includes death) and nature into his dismal condition of self-love and sterile introspection. This is one of Hawthorne's several treatments of the Wandering Jew legend that had struck his fancy indelibly.

—Darrell Abel, *The Moral Picturesque: Studies in Hawthorne's Fiction* (West Lafayette, Ind: Purdue University Press, 1988): pp. 304–306.

☙

EVAN CARTON ON CATHOLICISM AND THE WHITE LIGHT

[Professor of English at the University of Texas at Austin, Evan Carton is the author of several works on early American fiction, including *The Rhetoric of American Romance* and *Poe and Hawthorne*. He has also written articles on American writers from Emily Dickinson to John Irving, and on the role of history in literature. In this excerpt he analyzes the role of Catholicism in *The Marble Faun*.]

In *The Marble Faun* the desire for and the fear of intimate community, and the question of what constitutes a home, are again played out—this time much more directly—through the relationships of Hawthorne's characters to the ideas and the institutions of Catholicism. The home of the Catholic Church, of course, is Rome, but neither Hawthorne nor any of his characters is at home there. The early letters and notebook entries that Hawthorne wrote in Rome convey his acute sense of being in an alien environment; one entry, in fact, summarizes his impression of the city in the word *un-home-likeness.* ⟨ . . . ⟩

Hawthorne's novel can be seen to be built on this tension, this split, in the definition of home. "Home" in *The Marble Faun* is a contested territory to which America and Rome, Protestantism and Catholicism, middle-class marriage and the vocation of art, lay competing claims. The word itself appears again and again, most prominently in passages that represent the claims that Rome and Catholicism make on the allegiances of Hawthorne's American Protestants. Rome is called "this central home of the world" and "this home of art," and its universality is reinforced in its depictions as "the City of all time, and of all the world" and "the Eternal City." Similarly, the central monument of Catholicism, Saint Peter's, is described as religion's "material home" and, in the title of a chapter devoted to it, as "The World's Cathedral." (Throughout this novel, Hawthorne inaccurately refers to this historic church as a cathedral; the bishop's seat, or cathedral church of the pope as bishop of Rome, is in fact Saint John Lateran.)

The more closely we look at these phrases, the more suspicious we may become that they are subtle equivocations rather than endorsements. The same sentence that deems Rome "the Eternal City" and the "central home of the world" contrasts it with the "native homes in England or America" of the tourists who make up a large part of Rome's seasonal population. This comparison would suggest that Rome is the deeper and more spiritual home, yet its characterization as "the City of all time, and of all the world," may be read to imply the opposite: that Rome's claim is the claim of temporality, materiality, and worldliness rather than that of a "native" (in the sense of "original" or "essential") home. ⟨ . . . ⟩

Catholic Rome appears in *The Marble Faun* as the haunted home of Christianity. It is a city built around ruins and over corpses and haunted by the ghosts of its past, by ancient grandeur and ancient crimes. It is also a city that haunts its visitors. It cannot be fully known or possessed, yet it takes possession of those who enter it and makes its "bygone life," its alien history, more familiar and immediate to them than their own existences, which seem "but half as real, here, as elsewhere." As Hilda remarks: "I sometimes fancy . . . that Rome—mere Rome—will crowd everything else out of my heart." Hawthorne, like Hilda, finds Rome's and Catholicism's imperialistic claim on the emotions and imagination of the individual at once appealing and unacceptable. ⟨ . . . ⟩

One of *The Marble Faun*'s most frequent and important images symbolically enacts this judgment of Catholicism's multiplicity and indirection by linking the contest between Catholic Rome and Protestant America to questions of artistic form and value. This is the image of chromatic or prismatic light, which is invariably placed in opposition to pure, unrefracted, white light. An example, cited above, is Hawthorne's use of the stained-glass church window as a figure for Catholicism itself, a religion that offers "many painted windows, as it were, through which the celestial sunshine, else disregarded, may make itself gloriously perceptible." Several pages later, Kenyon confirms the implication that such glorious perceptibility is achieved at the cost of purity, simplicity, naturalness, and truth. Saint Peter's should not have any "ordinary panes of glass," he tells Hilda. "Daylight, in its natural state, ought not to be admitted here. It should stream through a brilliant illusion of Saints and Hierarchies, and old Scriptural images, and symbolized Dogmas, purple, blue, golden, and a broad flame of scarlet. Then, it would be just such an illumination as the Catholic faith allows to its believers. But, give me—to live and die in—the pure white light of Heaven!" Hilda, who has just succumbed to the relief of confession and senses the accusation in Kenyon's tones, replies: "I love the white light too!"

—Evan Carton, *The Marble Faun: Hawthorne's Transformations* (New York: Twayne Publishers, 1992): pp. 49–50, 52, 57.

Works by
Nathaniel Hawthorne

Fanshawe: A Tale. 1828

Twice-Told Tales. 1837

Famous Old People. 1840

Grandfather's Chair. 1841

Liberty Tree. 1841

Mosses from an Old Manse. 1846

The Scarlet Letter. 1850

The House of the Seven Gables. 1851

The Snow-Image, and Other Twice-Told Tales. 1851

True Stories from History and Biography. 1851

The Blithedale Romance. 1852

A Wonder-Book for Girls and Boys. 1852

The Life of Franklin Pierce. 1852

Tanglewood Tales for Girls and Boys. 1853

The Marble Faun. 1860

Our Old Home. 1863

Septimus Felton: or, The Elixir of Life. 1872

The Dolliver Romance and Other Pieces. 1876

Doctor Grimshawe's Secret. 1883

Works about
Nathaniel Hawthorne

Abel, Darrell. *The Moral Picturesque: Studies in Hawthorne's Fiction*. West Lafayette, Ind.: Purdue University Press, 1988.

Arvin, Newton. *Hawthorne*. Boston: Little, Brown, 1929.

Askew, Melvin W. "Hawthorne, the Fall, and the Psychology of Maturity." *American Literature* 34 (1962): 135–143.

Auerbach, Jonathan. *Romance of Failure: First Person Fictions of Poe, Hawthorne and James*. New York: Oxford University Press, 1989.

Baughman, Ernest. "Public Confession and *The Scarlet Letter*." *New England Quarterly* 40 (1967): 532–550.

Bayer, John G. "Narrative Techniques and the Oral Tradition in *The Scarlet Letter*." *American Literature* 52 (1980): 250–263.

Baym, Nina. *The Shape of Hawthorne's Career*. Ithaca, N.Y.: Cornell University Press, 1976.

Bell, Millicent. *Hawthorne's View of the Artist*. Albany, N.Y.: State University of New York Press, 1962.

Bewley, Marius. *The Complex Fate: Hawthorne, Henry James and Some Other American Writers*. London: Chatto and Windus, 1952.

Brodhead, Richard. *Hawthorne, Melville and the Novel*. Chicago: University of Chicago Press, 1976.

Charney, Maurice. "Hawthorne and the Gothic Style." *New England Quarterly* 34 (1961): 36–49.

Crowley, J. Donald. *Hawthorne: The Critical Heritage*. New York: Barnes and Noble, 1970.

Dauber, Kenneth. *Rediscovering Hawthorne*. Princeton: Princeton University Press, 1977.

Dryden, Edgar A. *Nathaniel Hawthorne: The Poetics of Enchantment*. Ithaca, N.Y.: Cornell University Press, 1977.

Easton, Alison. *The Making of the Hawthorne Subject*. Columbia: University of Missouri Press, 1996.

Feidelson, Charles, Jr. *Symbolism and American Literature*. Chicago: University of Chicago Press, 1953.

Garlitz, Barbara. "Pearl: 1850–1955." *PMLA* 72 (1957): 689–699.

Gollin, Rita K. *Nathaniel Hawthorne and the Truth of Dreams*. Baton Rouge: Louisiana State University Press, 1979.

Harding, Brian, ed. *Nathaniel Hawthorne: The Critical Assessments*. East Sussex: Helm Information, 1995.

Harris, Kenneth M. *Hypocrisy and Self-Deception in Hawthorne's Fiction*. Charlottesville: University Press of Virginia, 1988.

Hoffman, Daniel C. *Form and Fable in American Fiction*. New York: Oxford University Press, 1961.

Jones, E. Michael. *The Angel and the Machine: The Rational Psychology of Nathaniel Hawthorne*. Peru, Ill.: Sherwood Suyden, 1991.

Lawrence, D. H. *Studies in Classic American Literature*. New York: T. Seltzer, 1923.

Levin, Harry. *The Power of Blackness: Hawthorne, Poe, Melville*. New York: Alfred A. Knopf, 1958.

McCall, Dan E. "The Design of Hawthorne's 'Custom House.'" *Nineteenth-Century Fiction* 21 (1967): 349–358.

McPherson, Hugo. *Hawthorne as Myth-Maker: A Study in Imagination*. Toronto: University of Toronto Press, 1969.

Miller, J. Hillis. *Hawthorne and History: Defacing It*. Cambridge, Mass.: B. Blackwell, 1991.

Newberry, Frederick. *Hawthorne's Divided Loyalties: England and America in His Works*. Rutherford, N.J.: Fairleigh Dickinson University Press, 1987.

O'Conner, William Van. "Hawthorne and Faulkner: Some Common Ground." *Virginia Quarterly Review* 33 (1957): 105–123.

Pahl, Dennis. *Architects of the Abyss: The Indeterminate Fictions of Poe, Hawthorne and Melville*. Columbia: University of Missouri Press, 1989.

Pearce, Roy Harvey. *Hawthorne Centenary Essays*. Columbus: Ohio State University Press, 1964.

Rees, John O., Jr. "Hawthorne's Conception of Allegory: A Reconsideration." *Philological Quarterly* 54 (1975): 494–510.

St. Armand, Barton Levi. "Hawthorne's 'Haunted Mind': A Subterranean Drama of the Self." *Criticism* 13 (1971): 1–25.

Sandeen, Ernest. "*The Scarlet Letter* as a Love Story." *PMLA* 77 (1962): 425–435.

Shulman, Robert. "Hawthorne's Quiet Conflict." *Philological Quarterly* 47 (1968): 216–236.

Stubbs, John. *The Pursuit of Form: A Study of Hawthorne and the Romance.* Urbana: University of Illinois Press, 1978.

Turner, Arlin. *Nathaniel Hawthorne: A Biography.* New York: Oxford University Press, 1980.

Wagenknecht, Edward. *Nathaniel Hawthorne: The Man, His Tales, and Romances.* New York: Continuum, 1989.

Waggoner, Hyatt H. *Hawthorne: A Critical Study.* Cambridge: Harvard University Press, 1955.

Warren, Austin. *Rage for Order.* Ann Arbor: University of Michigan Press, 1959.

Warren, Robert Penn. "Hawthorne Revisited: Some Remarks on Hellfiredness." *Sewanee Review* 81 (1973): 75–111.

Index of
Themes and Ideas

NATHANIEL HAWTHORNE: biography of, 11–13; works about, 92–94; works by, 91

THE HOUSE OF THE SEVEN GABLES: aristocracy and democracy and, 49–50, 56–57; character types and, 51–52; characters in, 46–48; death in, 59–61, 61–62; ending of, 54–55; financial ruin and, 58–59; gothic convention and, 63–64; Hepzibah in, 58–59; historical context and, 49–50; hope and, 56–57; interior and exterior imagery in, 51–52, 63–64; irony in, 63–64; nature and, 54–55; Phoebe in, 61–62; plot of, 41–45; Poe and, 53; portraits in, 64–66; significance of the number seven in, 53; inherited sin and, 49–50; social ethics and, 49–50; Sophia Hawthorne and, 61–62; supernatural in, 59–61, 63–64, 64–66

THE MARBLE FAUN: art and experience in, 81–82; artist in, 83–84, 89–90; Catholicism and, 89–90; change in Donatello, 77–78; characters in, 72–74; Donatello in, 77–78, 85–87; Eden and, 77–78; eroticism and, 83–84; evil in, 81–82; Garden of Hilda in, 79–80; home and, 89–90; innocence in, 75–76; Kenyon in, 83–84; memory and, 87–88; plot of, 67–71; sin and, 77–78, 79–80; supernatural in, 87–88; time and, 75–76; time and history in, 87–88; virginity and, 79–80; white light in, 89–90

THE SCARLET LETTER: alchemy and, 26–28; Anne Hutchinson and, 35–37; appearance and, 39–40; characters in, 19–20; conflict in, 25–26; conscience and, 25–26; Dimmesdale in, 37–38, 39–40; elements of, 23–24; Faust and, 26–28; four states of being and, 31–33; Freud and, 33–35; guilt and, 30–31; humanity and, 31–33; immortality and, 31–33; justice and, 25–26; libido and, 33–35; nature in, 28–30, 31–33, 35–37; neurosis and, 33–35; Pearl and Chillingworth in, 30–31; penitence and, 33–35; plot of, 14–18; prison and, 35–37; puritanism and, 25–26; satire and, 21–22; selfishness and, 39–40; sex and, 35–37; symbolism in, 28–30, 30–31; symbolism of "A" in, 37–38; sympathy and, 21–22